AF814799

THE DOCTRINE OF NECESSITY
IN
INTERNATIONAL LAW

THE DOCTRINE OF NECESSITY IN INTERNATIONAL LAW

BY

BURLEIGH CUSHING RODICK

New York
COLUMBIA UNIVERSITY PRESS
1928

Copyright 1928
By COLUMBIA UNIVERSITY PRESS

Printed from plates. Published May 1928

Printed in the United States of America
Plimpton Press, Norwood, Mass.

TO

S. M. S.

WHOSE KINDNESS AND AID
DESERVE A FAR BETTER TRIBUTE

PREFACE

The subject of this study is described by its title — The Doctrine of Necessity in International Law. It has been the chief aim of the writer to discover the extent to which the doctrine of necessity in international law may be said to possess a certain amount of legal validity, and also the extent to which lawful limitations may be imposed upon its exercise. No attempt has been made to give a detailed account of the origin of the doctrine, or to discuss its philosophical and political aspects.

The writer owes much to the following members of the faculty of Columbia University: to Professor John Bassett Moore, for his encouragement and scholarly guidance; to Dr. Julius Goebel, Jr., who first suggested the topic and who rendered invaluable aid in its development; and to Professor Joseph P. Chamberlain, who gave freely of his time and scholarship in a careful revision of the entire manuscript.

The writer also desires to express his appreciation of the many favors he has received from the Columbia University Press; and he feels that he owes an especial debt of gratitude for the painstaking and scholarly editing of his manuscript by the editor of the Press, Dr. Clarke F. Ansley.

The writer has spent the greater part of five years in the preparation of this book. No one could be more conscious than he of its errors and imperfections, for which he alone assumes full responsibility. Nevertheless, as he ends his task, he finds himself strangely in sympathy with the words of Dr. Johnson: "I have protracted my work till . . . success and miscarriage are empty sounds: I therefore dismiss it with frigid tranquillity, having little to fear or hope from censure or from praise."

BURLEIGH CUSHING RODICK

NEW YORK CITY
February, 1928

CONTENTS

I

INTRODUCTION: VIEWS OF EARLY WRITERS

So far as the writer has been able to discover, no attempt has ever been made to deal critically and at length with the doctrine of necessity in international law. The books abound with references to "necessity," and it is often employed to excuse the commission of many acts in the field of international relations that might otherwise be open to question. Some writers on international law employ the word "necessity" to describe a condition which in their opinion has been the inevitable result of a series of antecedent facts. Others employ the term "political necessity" to describe those extraordinary and exceptional acts of a state which are committed in violation of the ordinary rights and duties imposed by international law on the ground that such action is essential to the welfare and preservation of the state committing the breach, and for which at the time of the commission of the act, no justification or excuse can be found in any well established principle of international law. Sometimes this act is a violation of an existing rule or treaty; sometimes it is an extension of the powers of the state into a field in which there are no existing rules of international law. Still other writers employ the term "legal necessity" to describe a situation in which a state claims and is granted the extraordinary and exceptional right to disregard the normal duty imposed upon it by a rule of international law when such action is essential to its preservation and continuity as a state. Some writers substitute the terms "political self-defense" and "legal self-defense" for the foregoing, — but no effort to differentiate the two sets of terms appears to have been made, with the result that they have become practically interchangeable in use. It is the main purpose of the writer to make a brief examination of the doctrine described by the terms "legal necessity," and "legal self-defense," with the further purpose of arriving at a greater precision in their definition and a more comprehensive understanding of their nature.

For the sake of analytical convenience we may divide those text-writers who have referred to the doctrine of necessity into two groups: — those who have dealt with it from the viewpoint of the so-called natural rights; and the historical writers who have recorded certain alleged instances of its practice without attempting to analyze these instances for the purpose of deducing rules of practice. References to the doctrine and statements to the effect that it was based upon "natural law" abound in the writings of the mediaeval lawyers and schoolmen; but these contributions to the subject are not important, for they were conceived before there was a general acceptance of the notion that the relations of political bodies were susceptible of legal regulation. These writers, in so far as they dealt with the idea of necessity, regarded its relation to private law; and there is, moreover, no positive proof that their statements exerted any important influence upon this later period in which the doctrine as we know it today actually arose. In fact, Hugo Grotius himself, "the father of international law," deserves, more than anyone else, to be considered the early founder of the doctrine of necessity. He attempted to explain its origin, to give illustrations of its practice among ancient states, and, — what is more remarkable, considering that by far the greater portion of his illustrations are drawn from the classical period, — he even gave a few illustrations of its practice in his own era. Finally, he endeavored to lay down some general rules for the purpose of imposing limitations upon its practice.

In dealing with the various forces which international law called into being, Grotius laid great stress upon the notion of necessity. His argument, in brief, is that, given certain premises of human impulse and external circumstances, man has been compelled to resort to certain rules. In addition to his general views as to the origin of the law, Grotius also laid stress upon the element of necessity in the operation of specific rules of law; and in this relation it is essential to note that to him the idea of necessity does not always imply the absence or denial of law but may under some circumstances be invoked to justify actions which otherwise would appear to be outside the pale of the law.

After dealing with the part played by necessity in the founding of the law of nations, Grotius proceeds to give numerous illustrations of the extent to which he conceives that a plea of necessity may lawfully be invoked. He points out that in time of peace the national jurisdiction is inviolable, subject to the following limitations which are based upon necessity: — The right to possess those things essential to life permits a people to pass through the territory of another state on the ground that necessity revives the common ownership of property which once existed,[1] and even gives them the right to reside there, provided they submit to its territorial laws.[2] The same principle permits a ship to make an involuntary entrance into the port of a foreign jurisdiction if forced to do so by stress of weather. As an example of a revival of this common ownership, he points out that "the Greeks who were with Xenophon, in their need took the ships which they found passing, spared the lading for its owners, fed and paid the sailors. This then is the first Right which, when ownership has been established, remains out of the old community of goods: namely, the Right of Necessity."[3] Thus necessity is held to justify the practice of angary. Here, also, Grotius is pointing out that necessity does not always result in the suspension of all law, but may result in the suspension of a particular rule and the revival of an older rule in its stead. Our modern idea of necessity, of course, rejects this view and studies the circumstances of the case.

Grotius's insistence upon the fundamental requirement of the independence of the state led him to emphasize the inviolability of the national jurisdiction. At the same time he indicated that circumstances of necessity may justify its extension. Thus for "the suppression of piracy and other crimes at sea . . . it was understood and declared of old, that the right of Holland and West Vriesland extended in every respect to the half-sea, or mid-water."[4]

Grotius devotes considerable attention to the problem of necessity in war. He admits that what we now call "military necessity" must exist in war, and he is even inclined to hold that the individual state itself must remain the final judge of the limits of its military needs: — ". . . it can scarcely be known by external indications, in a just war, what is the proper limit of self-defense, or recovery of property, or of exaction of punishment; so that it is by all means better, to leave this to the conscience of the belligerents than to appeal to extraneous decision."[5] Nevertheless he does endeavor to impose limits upon the will of the individual state by pointing out that the degree of military violence to be employed should not be in excess of actual military needs.[6]

He also makes several references to necessity in its relation to the law of neutrality. Subject to certain qualifications and limitations, he holds that military necessity will excuse the act of a belligerent in marching through the territory of a neutral state. This general right is deduced from the principle that property was placed in private hands with the understanding that circumstances of necessity would result in such a revival of common ownership as might be essential for the preservation of life;[7] and therefore "a transit is first to be requested; but if denied, may be asserted by force."[8] The right is, however, subject to the following limitations: — a request for a free passage should first be made;[9] the plea of necessity does not lie if the party making the request is engaged in an unjust war;[10] and proper safeguards and securities may be taken in order that no damage shall be committed.[11]

A similar situation exists in regard to the occupation of neutral territory and the seizure of neutral goods, due also to the fact that "in extreme necessity, the positive right of using things revives, as if they had remained common: for in all laws, and thus in the law of ownership, extreme necessity is excepted."[12] It therefore follows that "he who carries on a righteous war may lawfully seize a place situate in a land which is not at war; namely, if there be a danger not imaginary but certain, that the enemy will seize that place, and thence do irreparable damage: and next on condition that nothing can be taken which is not necessary for this purpose of caution, for example, the mere custody of the place, leaving to the true owner the jurisdiction and the revenues: finally, if it is done with the intention of restoring the custody of the true owner as soon as the necessity is over."[13]

It should be pointed out that Grotius in attempting to impose limitations upon the practice of necessity has at the same time opened many avenues which lead to its disregard. There can be little doubt that he is conscious of this result, because scattered here and there through his writings are repeated attempts to formulate rules for the purpose of imposing limitations upon the practice of the doctrine to which he has given his sanction. Nowhere in his work are these rules given a coherent and systematic presentation, and not infrequently do they abound in ambiguities and inconsistencies, but as nearly as they may be reduced to summary form, they indicate that Grotius felt that the doctrine of necessity ought to be subject to the following general limitations and qualifications: —

1. There must be an absence of *mens rea* on the part of one who exercises the alleged right.[14]

2. There must be a real and vital danger, either to life, or to property.[15]

3. The danger must be imminent in point of time.[16]

4. In seizing the property of neutrals the amount seized should be no greater than is necessary for the particular object in view.[17]

5. Consideration must be given to the equities involved. The plea of necessity, for example, cannot be admitted when the person against whom the action is directed is in an equal state of necessity himself.[18]

6. The person who has exercised the right is bound whenever possible to make restitution or give an equivalent to the owner.[19]

In raising the question of the extent to which Grotius permits necessity to contradict his rules of positive law, it may be suggested that it is possible that he saw in these rules a convenient outlet for forces that would otherwise be less subject of control. Such, at least, appears to be one of the motives that he himself assigns in explanation of his attitude.[20] It is not improbable that he felt it expedient to impose rules upon the general practice of necessity and at the same time permit it to be raised as a plea in a special and limited set of circumstances, feeling that in so doing he was imposing a check upon the general practice of the doctrine, which, if not absolutely perfect, was nevertheless — considering the character of the age and the circumstances under which he wrote — relatively best. It should be observed, finally, that except perhaps in the case of angary, these limited circumstances in which Grotius permits the plea of necessity to be raised relate chiefly to resistance to illegal acts and may therefore be classified as examples of excusable self-defense.

We have said that Grotius more than anyone else deserves to be considered the modern founder of the doctrine of necessity. This is true because of the amplitude with which he states the doctrine and the fact that he wrote in modern times. It should not, however, detract from the fact that Machiavelli, writing 115 years earlier, without aiming at a systematic presentation of the subject matter, and proceeding from entirely different premises, nevertheless had arrived at conclusions that bear a startling similarity to those of Grotius. The germ of the modern law of national jurisdiction, which in Italy owes a part of its development to Bartolus,[21] received at the hands of Machiavelli a realistic, and to some extent an opportunistic, expression in which it was not the old Roman law notions which were stressed, but considerations of expediency in the form of the doctrine of necessity. This doctrine was not unknown to the civilians, but due to its anomalous character, it naturally appealed to them far less as an argument for local autonomy among the Italian states than it did to a statesman and politician like Machiavelli. Believing as strongly as he did in such autonomy, it is not surprising that Machiavelli has given us a clear statement of the law of national jurisdiction and the right to defend it on the ground of necessity. In one of his diplomatic instructions he goes even farther and imposes a number of clear limitations upon the exercise of the right. This note deserves quotation at some length: —

" There has been a dispute, it seems, for some time, which may be at least very probably attended with bad consequences, betwixt the community of Vinca in your jurisdiction on one side, and the people of Fornole, who are subject to the Marquis of Massa, on the other, on account of Mount Rutainia . . . we hereby order you to acquaint the said Marquis as soon as possible, that you have a Commission from us to treat and confer with him in behalf of our subjects at Vinca, on the spot, concerning the lands in dispute, and after an ocular survey, and hearing the claims on both sides, to determine in a summary way, taking good care at the same time, however, to support the just rights of our subjects in a proper manner. But if he still persists in shuffling and evading a fair accommodation, as usual, and will come to no reasonable composition in favor of his people, but suffers them to use force and violence, as they have hitherto been accustomed to do, you are then (since it is lawful to repel force by force) to send for Grannesino, Captain of the batallion di Castigline, and employ the forces under his command to prevent our subjects at Vinca from having any further violence committed upon them, contrary to all justice and equity, taking heed to act rather upon the defensive than the offensive, and to support our people instead of attacking others. We would have you nevertheless in the first place, to make use of all gentle and persuasive arguments; according to your usual prudence, in order to bring about a fair and amicable adjustment of the matter." [22]

Here, then, is an early statement of the law of self-defense in its relation to the national jurisdiction: — the duty of a state to protect its subjects against the commission of an overt act by the subjects of a foreign jurisdiction, and to employ such a degree of force — but no more — as is necessary to repel the danger at hand. Considering the time of its composition and the fact that unrestricted violence is supposed to have been the rule of the day, this instruction emphasizing the requirement that action must be only defensory has some significance.

Machiavelli's writings contain a number of other references to the right of self-defense in international law. Thus he takes a position similar to the one later maintained by Grotius, that circumstances of exceptional necessity will warrant the expulsion of aliens.[23] In dealing with military necessity he declares that when "the entire safety of our country is at stake no consideration of what is just or unjust, merciful or cruel, praiseworthy or shameful, must intervene. On the contrary, every other consideration being set aside, that course alone must be taken which preserves the existence of the country and maintains its liberty."[24] He feels, however, that the influence of Christianity has tended to mitigate the former rigors of war and certain harsh practices that were formerly excused on the ground of military necessity.[25]

Machiavelli also holds that necessity may excuse the violation of neutrality when we have reason to suspect that the neutral is about to attack us,[26] but in view of the popular tradition that the policies of Machiavelli tend always to be unscrupulous, it is worthy of note that he declares it is far better to retain the good will of neutrals by justice and fair dealing.[27]

In estimating the part played by Machiavelli in developing the doctrine of necessity it is sufficient to repeat that he antedated Grotius by more than one hundred years in pointing out that in order to excuse the use of necessity, there must be a real danger to the life and property of the state and that the amount of force to be employed should be no greater than is essential to defend the particular rights in danger. It is sometimes said that a man is usually better than his philosophy, — at least he is generally capable of rising above it. Proof of this statement may be seen in the reactions of Grotius and Machiavelli toward the plea of necessity. Grotius, who, under the influence of natural law, began by denying it, had enough intellectual honesty to admit its existence; and Machiavelli, who, less under the influence of natural law, began by emphasizing it, had enough individual integrity to impose limitations upon its practice similar to those later imposed by Grotius. Thus by different routes both arrived at essentially the same conclusions. The moral and humane Grotius relied upon an appeal to natural law in order to find support for the limitations which he imposed upon the doctrine of necessity; while the realist, Machiavelli, placed similar limitations upon the law and founded them upon his own conscience and sense of justice. For the student of jurisprudence, however, there is no great distinction to be found between these two underlying ideas.

Our study of Machiavelli should logically be followed by an examination of Hobbes. He is, like Machiavelli, a great political realist and, as John Morley has pointed out in an illuminating essay, "He drew similar lessons from a similar experience."[28] In order to explain the attitude of Hobbes toward the doctrine of necessity we should begin with his famous statement that the law of nations and the law of nature are the same thing,[29] that every sovereign is in a state of nature toward every other sovereign.[30] From this it follows that every sovereign is compelled to exercise the right of self-defense against every other sovereign[31] for the purpose of protecting the national domain[32] and its essential boundaries.[33] Self-defense — and by this he means action induced by the force of circumstances — has dictated the acceptance of certain rules. Once the circumstances are favorable to a breach of the rule, the canons of self-defense laid down by Hobbes are a sufficient justification of such action. In other words, Hobbes finds the sanction of the law purely in objective facts — it is binding not because states will it to be but because circumstances compel it. This philosophy is the very apotheosis of the idea of necessity, but it promises no stability to the system it established, and for this reason the later jurists subjected it to a fierce rewriting.

In implying that military necessity will excuse the exercise of harsh measures in time of war provided they result in a military advantage commensurate with their severity, Hobbes is making an early statement of a rule that has since been adopted by many writers on military necessity: — "It is a proverbial saying," he declares, "that *inter arma silent leges*. There is little therefore to be said concerning the laws that men are to observe one towards another in time of war, wherein every man's being and well-being is the rule of his actions. Yet thus much the law of nature commendeth in war: that men satiate not the cruelty of their present passions, whereby in their own conscience they foresee no benefit to come. For that belongeth not to a necessity, but a disposition of the mind to war, which is against the law of nature."[34] In this way the Machiavellian idea is given the natural law benediction.

Hobbes also has a few words to say in regard to the part played by military necessity in its relation to conquest and the termination of hostilities. He holds that necessity will excuse the private citizen in submitting to the enemy when his sovereign is unable to protect him, and the soldier when his sovereign is unable to maintain him as a military unit in the field.[35] Thus the essential point to note is that with

Grotius, Machiavelli, and Hobbes, military necessity is used to justify and excuse the release from a normal obligation — the normal duty of states toward each other in the case of Grotius and Machiavelli, and the normal duty of the subject toward the sovereign in time of war in the case of Hobbes.

The influence of Hobbes upon the development of the doctrine of necessity is of considerable importance. By his emphasis upon the fact that commonwealths were in a state of nature towards each other, he established the doctrine of necessity, at the outset, at least, firmly upon the basis of its relation to the necessities of the state; but the extent to which these state necessities would be recognized by international law remained a matter for future development.

Our examination of Hobbes should logically be followed by a study of Pufendorf. Not only does he openly acknowledge the debt that he owes to the former, but it is evident from an analysis of his work, that much of his treatise, *On the Law of Nature and of Nations,* is an adaptation and elaboration of Hobbesian ideas. Owing to the fact that he was writing at a time when it was a part of the literary and scholastic tradition for men to find the explanation of most human activities in terms of what they believed to be instituted or natural propensities, it was more or less inevitable that he should deal with the problem from this purely hypothetical and quasi-rationalistic angle. Thus from the very beginning of his theory he links up necessity and the impulse of self-preservation. "The case of necessity," he says, "is a thing in everybody's mouth, and the force of it is generally acknowledged in the world. Hence we commonly say that it hath no law, that 'tis a supposed or presumptive exception to all human ordinances or constitutions; and that therefore it gives a right of doing many things otherwise forbidden."[36] Pufendorf seems to feel that the solution of this apparent dilemma is antecedent to the establishment of any sound legal system and he does his best to master it.

He begins his treatise by essaying what he conceives to be primarily an historical explanation of the origin of law. If we take this view of his system it will explain the apparent duality of his ideas — the clash between his arrant determinism on the one hand and his attempt to rationalize the behavior of men on the other. His determinism is responsible for a conception of necessity and self-defense in which he holds that men are, by the inherent constitution of their being, forced to take such measures as they feel are essential for their own protection, — and in general, he holds that the same principle applies to states. He realizes, on the other hand, that there are circumstances so exceptional in their nature that the ordinary forces which impel men to follow the course that he has predetermined for them, are quite overcome by the force of extraordinary facts. He therefore develops at some length his theory of necessity as a justification and excuse for the disregard of law, — and here we come to the second aspect of his views on necessity, for Pudendorf is really using the idea of necessity in a double sense. On the one hand he employs it loosely for the purpose of giving what he conceives to be an historical explanation of certain developments; but, on the other hand, it is obvious that he does not intend to convey the impression that the sort of necessity which impels a man to accept a rule that he shall not kill, is similar to the necessity which impels him in self-defense to violate the rule. The latter, it is clear, is far different from the former.

In dealing with this second type of necessity, and the one with which we are primarily concerned, he holds that it is exceptional in its nature and that it ought to be considered in the light of an excuse;[37] that it is not to be employed unless there is an actual danger [38] that is imminent in point of time, and that may not otherwise be avoided, unless the act of avoidance itself tends to put him who exercises it in greater need of self-defense than he was prior to its exercise.[39] He also points out that there must be a lack of opportunity to apply to a magistrate for protection,[40] due to some of the circumstances already mentioned, such as the imminence of danger, or because the danger has occurred in a place beyond the magistrate's jurisdiction.[41] He declares that the principle may be exercised in defense of life, or property essential to life,[42] and in cases of dire extremity it may be extended to include the requisition of private property belonging to another from whom we have suffered no harm,[43] and the destruction of his goods,[44] provided restitution be made.[45] The amount of force to be employed in these cases, however, should be no more than is barely essential for the defense of the particular rights involved.

It is true that Pufendorf makes no direct application of these rules of necessity and self-defense to the law of nations. Superficially, these rules which are derived from the law of nature are to be considered mainly in connection with their application to internal law. On the other hand, we must bear in mind that Pufendorf drew no distinction between the law of nature and the law of nations but said they were the same thing. It therefore follows that in his subsequent discussion of necessity in its relation to international law, there is a tendency to impose a similar set of limitations upon its operation. Proof of this may be seen by a brief examination of the cases in which the problem is presented.

In dealing with necessity in its relation to the national jurisdiction he declares that a state may defend itself by extending its jurisdiction over its marginal seas to such a point as it may deem essential for the protection of its fisheries and maritime rights, provided that in so doing it does not infringe upon the national rights that belong to other states.[46] He also deals at length with the problem of necessity in its relation to the right of the national jurisdiction to make a free passage through neutral territory. He appears to consider this question to be of the utmost practical importance and it seems reasonable to infer that he was influenced to take this view by the course of certain international events. In 1667 he had published a work in which he had made a critical analysis of the government of the Empire and had arrived at the conclusion that it was essentially a union of independent states.[47] During the years, 1670–72, he wrote and published his *De jure naturae et gentium.* These years also constitute one of the most critical periods in the entire history of the Empire. In 1668 the Triple Alliance had compelled Louis XIV to sign the Treaty of Aix-la-Chapelle and temporarily abandon his attempt to conquer the Spanish Netherlands; but in reality the next four years was a period in which Louis was making strenuous efforts to renew the struggle by breaking up the Triple Alliance, negotiating the so-called secret treaty of Dover with Charles II, and isolating Holland. In 1672 he again declared war, and this so alarmed Emperor Leopold that he made an alliance with the Elector Frederick William of Brandenburg and the States General of Holland to oppose these new aggressions. The states of the Empire near the Low Countries were in serious danger[48] and it would appear that Pufendorf was confronted with the problem of devising a scheme by which the states of the Empire would be able to defend themselves against the impending invasion; and at the same time of interpreting the rules of international law involved in such a way as to leave these states free to advance a plea of necessity in extenuation and excuse for any invasion of foreign territory that they themselves should deem it necessary to make.

Pufendorf takes pains to point out at the beginning that he disagrees with Grotius in regard to the latter's theory that circumstances of necessity may justify a free passage through a revival of common ownership that once existed.[49] His attitude, on the other hand, amounts practically to a weighing of the equities presented by the need of the national jurisdiction to defend itself against the potential dangers of the grant, and the right of the petitioning state to demand the grant if circumstances of necessity require it. Thus he points out that circumstances of necessity and self-defense may require that the national jurisdiction refuse to grant a passage when such an act would tend to constitute a violation of a right of neutrality against a third state and thus provoke its enmity; [50] or when such a grant is liable to precipitate a war within its borders.[51] On the other hand he declares that the state making the request has the right to receive the grant for the transportation of goods that " are absolutely necessary for the support of life " ; [52] or in the case of " necessity, or . . . some extraordinary advantage, when it would be inhumanity in the other party, not to comply. . . ." [53]

One thing in this relation is worthy of note. Pufendorf, although he may have had the matter tacitly in mind, seems to place no great stress upon the fact that the breach of a rule of law is involved in most of these cases and that this is a consideration which should be taken into account in weighing the equities. We have pointed out that the situation was a matter of vital concern to the peace of Europe, and Pufendorf looking upon it realistically, regarded the exigencies of the moment as alone governing. In other words, he does not postulate the problem thus: A rule exists; do circumstances justify its suspension, or excuse its violation? but rather: An emergency has arisen; what course is proper under the circumstances? This difference of approach is not, moreover, merely academic. The first method premises a legal system observed with some degree of regularity. The latter premises nothing and throws the relations of state into a chaos. Pufendorf, however, is not to be too severely censured for an attitude which is the result of the times in which he lived. His argument discloses the tenuous hold that the law had upon states at that time and an attempt to make the best of the situation by laying down a rule of expediency if not of law.

In view of the fact that at the time Pufendorf wrote, there can be no doubt that the right to resort to reprisals was regarded as a rule of law,[54] it is somewhat surprising to find that he holds that acts of reprisal and retorsion are exceptional in their nature and are only to be justified in exceptional circumstances.[55] This is doubtless due to the fact that he was influenced by the humanitarian spirit which had moved Grotius and that such non-amicable modes of redress scarcely fitted into his world of carefully balanced rights. Then, too, his opinion was doubtless influenced by the situation in the Empire, where, as we have already observed, a multitude of petty states were endeavoring to stay aloof from the devastating wars of the period and were subjected to all manner of violence in the name of law, against which they were unable to defend themselves.

Pufendorf's explanation of the philosophical basis of military necessity is interesting and worth repeating:— "For a state of war as such, hath no other measure of action but force . . . [and] when it is necessary we should defend or assert our rights, where they are not to be obtained by peaceable means, we ought to think that the shortest way to the attainment of that end is the most agreeable to nature. And therefore since by compacts that tend only to moderate and qualify hostilities, the war is only drawn out to greater length; 'tis evident they must be contrary to nature." [56] This amounts practically to saying that military necessity, in relation to acts directed against belligerents, is without limits, nor does he shrink from this conclusion: — "For a state of hostility in itself gives a man unlimited liberty to take all the advantages he can against his enemy." [57] It is true that he later declares that men "ought to be particularly careful, that as far as possible, and their own necessary defense and future security will permit, to proportion the evils they inflict upon their enemy, to the measures and moderation observed by civil courts in punishing criminals and offenders." [58] But in using the saving clause, "their own necessary defense and security," it would appear that he recognized that his humanitarian ideas were little more than the expression of a pious hope of what might be rather than a statement of what the law actually was. This is clear from the list of specific instances which follow, in which he excuses the exercise of military necessity. Thus he agrees with Grotius that military necessity makes it "lawful for him who wages a just war, to possess himself of a place seated in a country that is at peace with him: if there be certain (and not only imaginary) danger, that the enemy will otherwise surprise it, and from thence assail him with irreparable mischief.[59] It will be observed that Pufendorf is here using a plea of military necessity to justify a belligerent in the seizure of a place within a country with which he is at peace. It is the only case in which he employs the plea to justify a violation of neutral rights; but even in this situation he declares that the seizor must be "certain" that the enemy is about to occupy the place and thus do the belligerent irreparable damage. This would seem to show that Pufendorf intended to impose strict limits upon belligerent action in such a case in order that it might not become a convenient excuse for the violation of neutral rights. Military necessity will also excuse the violation of a parole,[60] the sacrifice of hostages by the state that gave them,[61] and the use of bribes,[62] stratagem and fraud.[63]

The limitations imposed by Pufendorf upon the general exercise of the doctrine of necessity are, as in the case of Grotius, indefinite, and for that reason, difficult to determine. Such as they are, they have already been indicated in connection with our examination of the general nature of his theory.[64] It is, however, an open question as to whether his treatment of the problem marks an actual advance toward a legal analysis of the problem. He did, it is true, take a step in that direction by discarding the anthropomorphic conception of sovereignty held by Grotius, and the abstract, metaphysical conception held by Hobbes. He also sensed more clearly than his predecessors that the plea of necessity arises as the result of an exceptional series of circumstances and that in such a situation consideration should be given to the conflicting equities involved. On the other hand, in seeking to avoid some of the pitfalls made by these earlier writers, he fell into another: — he based his doctrine of necessity upon that element of human reason which he held to be inherent in natural law; and since later writers adopted this principle and held that human reason was a factor of universal validity, the net result of his work was to leave the doctrine of necessity still more strongly entrenched in the mire of natural law and to make confusion worse confounded.

Nor did the so-called writers on natural law who succeeded Pufendorf do anything to improve the situation. Their contribution amounts to little more than a repetition of the arguments already advanced by Grotius, Machiavelli, Hobbes and Pufendorf. Rousseau (1712–78), to be sure, endeavors to impose limitations upon the exercise of military necessity by declaring that "war does not give a right to do anything beyond what is absolutely necessary to its end, that is, to the subduing of a hostile power";[65] but this is merely the negative statement of a positive rule to the effect that it does give a right to do anything which is necessary to subdue a hostile power. It may, nevertheless, be doubted if this rule, in either its negative or its positive form, is of very great practical value. Wolff (1679–1754) repeats the argument of Grotius and Hobbes that the law of self-defense requires that each nation continue to be the judge of the necessities of its own preservation and the duties that it owes to other states.[66] Vattel (1714–67) repeats the theory of Grotius and Pufendorf to the effect that necessity may be responsible for the temporary repeal of the existing civil law and the revival of an earlier rule of natural law in its place.[67] He also repeated at length the theory of Pufendorf to the effect that in the case of conflicting necessities there should be a careful weighing of the equities involved.[68] It is only in dealing with the problem of military necessity that Vattel makes a slight contribution to the problem by the objective manner in which he deals with certain facts. Vattel declares that the plea of military necessity may be employed to excuse the action of the states of Western Europe in making war against the Turks without a declaration. At first glance this may appear to resemble the position taken by Grotius to the effect that the rules of international law did not apply to heathen states. But Grotius excluded the Turks because they were not Christians; Vattel, because of more realistic reasoning to the effect that: — "The Turks imprison and even maltreat the ambassadors of those Powers with which they have decided to go to war; it would be running a great risk for a herald to go into their midst to declare war. Their cruelty releases a state from the necessity of sending them." [69] This, strangely enough, foreshadows a current theory to the effect that the doctrine of necessity will excuse the action of certain states in the use of exceptional measures in their dealings with lawless and unorganized communities on the ground that such action constitutes an essential measure of international police. This important development of the problem will be examined in some detail in connection with our study of intervention.

The work of Vattel virtually marks the end of these writers on international law who based their doctrines upon the so-called natural rights. Any study of the views of early writers in regard to the doctrine of necessity would, however, be incomplete without a brief glance at some of the members of the so-called historical school. By this group we refer to those writers on international law who show a stronger tendency than did the exponents of the so-called natural law to rely upon the presentation of a series of objective and dynamic events, which in their opinion were largely instrumental in shaping the actual course of the international relations which they were endeavoring to portray. It must, however, be confessed at the outset, that in spite of the fact that their general method of approach to the problems of international law was relatively more scientific than that of the so-called natural law writers, nevertheless their discussion of the doctrine of necessity adds little if anything to the data presented by the former group. Albericus Gentilis (1552–1608), the so-called founder of the historical school, gives a detailed discussion of one case in which the problem was actually a point at issue. Beyond this, however, there is little to be found.

The case discussed by Gentilis deals with "an English Ship which Fought with a Tuscan Ship and was Captured." Each party entered a plea of self-defense, and Gentilis, instead of relying upon the general rules of natural law, endeavors to make a concrete analysis of the case at hand in the following words: —

1. ". . . he is presumed to be the aggressor who thought that he had suffered some wrong." Gentilis concludes that "the Tuscan might have thought he was being wronged by the commerce of England with the Turks."

2. "He is presumed to be the aggressor who is stronger than his opponent." Gentilis adds that "the Tuscan ship was stronger than our merchant vessel."

3. "He is presumed to be the aggressor who is accustomed to brawl and who carries weapons." Gentilis implies that the Tuscan was a fighting ship but that the English ship was a merchant vessel.

4. ". . . that person is presumed to be the aggressor who, besides fitting the hypotheses just mentioned is the victor."

5. "He who gave the challenge to battle and to wrath is held to have begun it," and Gentilis adds that "even the verdict recites that the Tuscan vessel fired two broadsides first."

6. "Or suppose that the offense of the Tuscans was justified also. At least in the doubtful conflict between a justified offense and a justified defense there is no one who will not give such a beneficent defense the preference over offense. The more just surpasses the just, the more equitable the equitable, the more beneficent, and the more just is given the preference over the just." [70]

It will be seen that the rules laid down by Gentilis, and especially his attempt to weigh the equities in such a way that greater necessities shall prevail over the lesser, resemble the principles laid down by the writers on natural law. The value of this analysis of Gentilis, therefore, does not lie so much in his presentation of the rules themselves as in his manner of their application: — not infrequently the so-called writers on natural law confined their discussion of the problem to abstract situations, or to cases that arose in private law, or to half-mythical situations that arose among ancient states; but in the case observed above, Gentilis is dealing with an actual instance in which the plea of self-defense was employed to excuse conduct that occurred between two states in the early modern era.

The successor of Gentilis in the English historical school was Sir Richard Zouche (1590–1661). In discussing the question of "whether Elizabeth . . . justly assumed the protection of the Netherlands against the King of Spain," he declares that "fearing . . . lest the power of the Spaniard might spread more dangerously than ever in territories which were almost contiguous to her own realm and conveniently situated for effecting an invasion of England, she resolved . . . to take thought for the safety of the people committed to her charge by frustrating the machinations of her enemies. Accordingly she openly undertook the protection of the Netherlands." [71] Here, then, is a discussion of another case of alleged necessity in modern times, in which the writer intimates that the need of defending the national jurisdiction against a potential attack may excuse an act of intervention to prevent its consummation.

Among the German historical writers, Rachel (1628–91) and Textor (1638–1701) merely repeat the arguments of Grotius.[72] Bynkershoek (1673–1743), in laying down his famous rule of the three-mile limit, emphasizes the fact that the nature of self-defense and the extent to which it may be employed will vary from time to time with the nature and range of the weapons employed; [73] but this is little more than a repetition of the statement made by the natural law writers to the effect that the amount of force to be employed shall be determined by the amount required to subdue the enemy.[74] A similar repetition is made by Montesquieu (1689–1755) in his statement that there must be a proportion between the defenses of a state and its actual defensive needs,[75] and by G. F. von Martens (1756–1821) in his statement that "every sovereign is obliged to confine himself to the employment of the lowest degree by which he can obtain satisfaction."[76] He also declares that "if a sovereign sees himself menaced with an attack, he may take up arms in order to ward off the blow, and may even commence the exercise of those violences that the enemy is preparing to exercise against him, without being chargeable with having begun an offensive war."[77] This resembles the position taken by Zouche to the effect that the plea of necessity may be employed to excuse an act of intervention, except that it is also extended to include a general state of belligerency. He also gives a definite illustration of what he maintains is justifiable military necessity. He declares that "except in cases of necessity, it is now admitted that the besiegers ought to direct their artillery against the fortifications only, and not, intentionally, against the public edifices, or any other buildings, either within or without the ramparts"; but he adds that: — "There are cases, however, which justify the besieger in threatening to burn the public edifices, for instance to deter the besieged from making signals from the towers or steeples, by the tolling of bells, etc. This was done formerly much oftener than in our day. We find one instance of it at the siege of Vienna by the Turks."[78] It is believed that von Martens has in this passage correctly stated a portion of the law of military necessity as it now applies to bombardments.

Our brief account of the historical writers may well close with von Martens, since those who have followed him have contributed little of value. In reviewing the work of the historical writers as a whole, it may be said that while they made no great advance beyond the theoretical writers in their analysis of necessity, it may nevertheless be said that they helped to pave the way for a more rational and scientific consideration of the problem. In the cases cited from Gentilis, Zouche, and von Martens it will be observed that there is a marked tendency among the historical writers to return to the rationalism of Machiavelli, and to insist upon the principle that the doctrine of necessity is the product, not of theoretical conceptions, but of facts in the actual world of international relations. In this way the historical writers helped to emphasize the truth of the statement that any correct analysis of the problem of necessity should be based upon actual cases illustrative of its use. In the succeeding chapters the writer aims to make such an examination in some detail.

II

NECESSITY AND THE NATIONAL JURISDICTION

The doctrine of necessity in its relation to topics of concern to the national jurisdiction may be discussed from the viewpoints of necessity in its relation to the national jurisdiction and its territorial limits, and necessity in its relation to the national jurisdiction and its legal effects. The problem of necessity in its relation to the territorial limits of the national jurisdiction deals largely with necessity in its relation to the so-called " marginal seas " — those waters, gulfs, straits, bays, rivers, roadsteads, ports, arms of the sea, and contiguous islands which border upon the maritime state, and over which it exercises a certain measure of control. The leading objects for which the maritime state may exercise this measure of control over its marginal seas are the protection of its fisheries, the establishment and enforcement of its revenue, inspection, sanitation, and hovering acts, the suppression of piratical acts and the enforcement of neutrality — although the extent of its sovereign rights is doubtless not limited to these objects. It is true that such acts are based upon necessity in the general sense of the term, but it is also true that in most cases these acts now constitute a normal operation of the law of territorial inviolability and are not based upon necessity of the exceptional kind which we have primarily in view. The problem of exceptional necessity would arise, however, in connection with a violation of the existing rules in regard to the territorial limits of the national jurisdiction and the plea that such a violation should be excused because of the exigencies of the particular situation. The question of whether the rule shall yield to a new exception is to be determined by the conflicting needs of the littoral state on the one hand, and the needs of all the states for a free sea on the other, — the propinquity of the littoral state tending to lend to its claims a certain presumptive value which must be overcome by evidence that the claims would work an actual damage to the general interests of the body of states. If the exception were to be established, it would then have all the force and validity of the rule. We are here concerned, however, chiefly with the cases in which a single act occurs in violation of the rule and the plea of necessity is raised in excuse. In that case a state must be able to show that the emergency confronting it was so great that no other course could have reasonably been adopted.

Cases in which the plea of exceptional necessity has been raised in connection with the national jurisdiction and its territorial limits are not infrequent, but they have also tended to give rise to questions of even greater import than the territorial limits of the national jurisdiction. It therefore follows that those cases of exceptional necessity dealing with fisheries and the establishment and enforcement of revenue, inspection, sanitation and hovering acts, may more logically be associated with exceptional necessity in its relation to the national jurisdiction; necessity and piratical acts may be dealt with in connection with necessity and the high seas; and necessity and the enforcement of neutrality is a part of the general problem of necessity in its relation to neutrality and will be so considered.

The plea of necessity has at times been advanced to excuse the action of the state in extending its control over the fisheries that extend along its marginal seas. Here again, however, these cases would appear to involve the normal operation of a legal right rather than cases of exceptional need to be excused on the plea of self-defense. These claims to an extensive jurisdiction may be divided into three classes: — claims based on physical conditions such as those that prevail in Norway; claims based on economic considerations of a relatively permanent character; and claims of a temporary character based upon allegations of a temporary necessity. The claim of Norway, for example, that she should have exclusive rights over all her fjords, on the ground that the three-mile limit would be impracticable owing to the physical configuration of the coast-line and on the ground that the possession of these fisheries is of vital importance to her people, would appear to be the exercise of a normal right rather than an exceptional action to which she should be required to make a plea in justification and excuse.[79] The situation would appear to be similar in the case of economic considerations of a permanent character. Thus a state would appear to have a normal and not exceptional right to extend its coastal jurisdiction beyond the three-mile limit in order to include certain so-called sedentary fisheries which lie upon the ocean's bed. Usually they are so situated that the adjacent state alone can make use of them, and in *The Apollo* it was declared that they were the product of its soil and were therefore subject to the same rules of self-defense that apply to the state itself.[80] It is evident, however, that the word " self-defense " was here used in a normal and not exceptional sense. So, too, in the case of the North Atlantic Fisheries: — The Hague Tribunal agreed with Great Britain that " conditions of national and territorial integrity, of defense, of commerce and industry are vitally concerned with the control of the bays penetrating the national coast-line," [81] — but this is another declaration of a normal and not exceptional right. Claims of a temporary character based upon a passing need may sometimes contain illustrations of the type of necessity which we have primarily in mind; but even here the question must be raised as to whether the action of the state does not constitute the exercise of a normal right. Thus the action of the national juridiction in defending its marginal fisheries by means of hot pursuit, while undoubtedly based upon the right of self-defense, would appear to be the exercise of a lawful right, and not an exceptional action for which a special plea of necessity must be made in excuse.[82] The Bering Sea controversy, on the other hand, is a case in which the plea of exceptional necessity was definitely made. The tribunal held, however, that the action of the United States in using force against the Canadian vessels engaged in pelagic sealing was not to be excused on the ground that it constituted an exceptional case of necessity and self-defense. The suggestion of the tribunal that restrictions should be imposed upon the taking of the seals upon the high seas and in the vicinity of the Pribilof Islands, and that the use of firearms in killing them should be prohibited, should be interpreted not as a recognition of, or concession to the plea of exceptional necessity presented by the United States, but merely as a recognition of the fact that the United States had a normal right to be protected in the pursuits of its legitimate share of an interest. The United States failed to establish its plea of necessity because it was unable to establish its claim to property in the seals while these seals were upon the high seas; and even if it had been able to establish this claim, the degree of force which it had employed was in excess of current needs in the sense that greater efforts should have first been exerted in the direction of a peaceful settlement.[83] It may therefore be said that the plea of exceptional necessity will not ordinarily excuse the act of a state in seeking to extend its marginal seas for the protection of its fisheries. In order for such a plea to constitute a justification and excuse, the right of fishing must first be established, and it must also be established that the measures adopted were the sole ones at the disposal of the state and were in fact essential for the protection of its property.

The plea of exceptional necessity in its relation to the national jurisdiction and its legal effects has also arisen in connection with police and other regulations, jurisdiction over ports, involuntary entrance, inviolability of territory, the duty to restrain injurious agencies, and extraterritorial crime. Circumstances of exceptional necessity will excuse the national jurisdiction in adopting measures of unusual severity if they are necessary to enforce its port regulations and its laws and regulations in regard to quarantine that are in turn of vital importance to its own security and self-preservation. Thus in the case of the French passenger steamer, *La France*, which was fired upon by the harbor authorities at Bahia, the Government of Brazil declared that " the damage done the vessel and the death of the passenger was the result of systematic disobedience of port regulations on the part of commanders of foreign packets and of utter disregard for the signals from the gunboat, which were duly given in the case; that the only way to prevent the introduction of disease from foreign ports was to subject vessels coming from those ports to rigid inspection before entering the inner harbor, and the only way to compel them to stop, when they disregarded the signals, was to fire on them with shot. The claim of the Italian Government in behalf of the passenger killed was likewise rejected. Claims made by English companies for firing upon their vessels under circumstances similar to the above were not entertained by the foreign office." [84]

The case cited above helps to make plain an important distinction. In the Bering Sea controversy it may be said that an abnormal situation had resulted in exceptional action on the part of the United States. But the chief reason for the rejection of the plea of necessity in that case was the fact that the action taken could not be said to be in defense of a clearly acknowledged right. In the case of Brazil, however, the plea of necessity was employed in the defense of an acknowledged right. It is true that the right was enforced by abnormal means, but the lawful character of the right combined with the circumstances of the case constituted an excuse.

The fact that the state may exercise jurisdiction over its ports is largely a normal right based upon its right to maintain peace and security therein. Nevertheless, in so doing the state may at times resort to certain exceptional measures in connection with foreign ships of war. Thus, "if . . . the captain of a vessel were to allow political refugees to maintain communication with the shore and to make the ship a focus of intrigue, or if he were to send a party of marines to arrest a deserter, an extreme case would arise, in which the imminence of danger, in the one instance, and in the other the disregard of the sovereign rights of the state, would justify the exceptional measure of expulsion."[85] It is true that Marshall in The Schooner *Exchange* v. McFadden [86] declared that ships of war were exempt, but he specifically stated that the exemption was confined to such time as the ship is "demeaning herself in a friendly manner." Not only may the territorial authority use force to prevent or put an end to a violation of neutrality by a foreign ship of war, but if it undertakes to commit any act of aggression or of hostility whatever, such a situation will excuse the action of the territorial state in employing all the measures that may be required for a legitimate defense.[87] Such an action might be considered the exercise of a normal right of sovereignty if it were not for the fact that it is a radical departure from normal conditions; and that the national jurisdiction in making its plea of justification and excuse for the exercise of such exceptional measures should, from the standpoint of international law, be required to present evidence to show that such a situation of necessity did in fact exist as to excuse the measures taken in defense.

The plea of exceptional necessity will also excuse the action of a vessel in making an involuntary entrance in the case of stress of weather,[88] lack of vital materials in the form of equipment, provisions, water and fuel,[89] and in the case of pursuit by pirates and enemies.[90] It may perhaps be argued that such entrances do not constitute a breach of the law as long as they comply with the tests that have been more or less definitely laid down by the courts — such, for example, as the rule that the burden of proof must rest upon the person setting up the plea,[91] that the necessity must be real and not imaginary,[92] and that it must be genuine and not tainted with collusion and fraud.[93] It may be argued that where the facts constitute sufficient justification, an involuntary entrance may be defended as a normal right. But the weight of authority does not appear to support such an analysis of the situation. The plea must first be presented in justification and excuse and it is not until it is accepted that entrance is excused. The very fact that the ship making the entrance must prove that such necessity existed is proof that the right to enter is permitted if the facts to justify the entrance can be established. In other words, the right to enter is clear but in order for a ship to avail itself of the right, it must show that the necessity existed in fact.

The plea of exceptional necessity has at times been employed to excuse the action of a national jurisdiction in landing forces within the borders of another national jurisdiction for the purpose of protecting the lives and property of its nationals when the authorities are unable or unwilling to furnish such protection. This topic will be considered in some detail in connection with necessity as an excuse for intervention; it is therefore at this point sufficient to say that a state is not bound to provide absolute protection for the persons and property of foreign nationals and that only circumstances of an exceptional nature in the form of a vital danger to the life and property of the state — a danger so exceptional in its nature that interposition of a more peaceful nature will be of no avail — will furnish an excuse for intervention in their behalf. It is believed that the proposition was stated correctly by the American Government in writing to its minister in Corea, when in answer to a request for military protection, it declared that "while the Department does not wish to in any way forbid you calling on the commander of the United States naval force on the Asiatic station for protection when in your judgment such is imperatively demanded, it does wish to discourage, so far as possible, such practice." [94]

Circumstances of exceptional necessity may, however, excuse the action of a national jurisdiction in time of peace in repelling a sudden attack originating within the territory of one jurisdiction and taking effect within the territory of another. This is the problem raised by such cases as the various invasions of Spanish Florida by the United States in 1812, 1814, and 1817–18,[95] the invasion of Mexico by the United States in 1836,[96] and the Caroline Affair.[97] The plea of exceptional necessity may rightfully be employed to excuse the action of the invaded state in using force to repel such an attack. It is true that in so doing it is in turn forced to violate the sovereignty of the state responsible for the attack; but such a violation may be made the subject of an excuse because the state that receives it has not only compelled the first state to act in self-defense; but it is also held directly responsible for the first violation, and indirectly responsible for the violation which it suffers in return, which results from the first, because it had knowledge of the condition that produced the first violation and through sufferance permitted it to continue. It is therefore charged with knowledge of, and responsibility for, the direct and indirect results of its own acts.

The plea of exceptional necessity has also been advanced to excuse the action of a state in adopting extraordinary measures to repel an injurious agency and pursue dangerous marauders beyond its borders. It is believed that circumstances of such a nature may arise that the plea of necessity may rightfully be employed to excuse such action. Thus, for example, in 1877 orders were given the military authorities of the United States to cross the Mexican border, if necessary in pursuit of lawless raiders.[98] The Mexican Government protested against these orders,[99] but the United States justified them as necessary because of the conditions that then existed on the border.[100] Subsequently, in 1882, an agreement was concluded between the two countries providing for the reciprocal right of pursuit of such marauders by the armies of both countries. Evidence of the fact that the United States considered such an exercise of power without a prior treaty agreement to be exceptional and unusual may be seen in its discussion of a similar problem with Great Britain with reference to the Canadian border. The American minister at London was requested to ask the British Government for permission to cross the Canadian border in pursuit of marauding Indians, but he was directed " distinctly " to " admit " that the United States did " not claim as a right that its armed forces shall in any case cross the frontier," and he was also requested to state that the concession if made would be subject to such restraints and guarantees as would prevent any possible abuse.[101] It is believed that, subject to such limitations, the plea of necessity might be considered in lawful justification and excuse for such action.

The plea of necessity has also been employed to excuse the action of a state in assuming criminal jurisdiction over aliens in respect of acts not committed within its territory. Many authorities have denied that the plea of necessity may thus be employed, but the weight of precedent and authority appear to point to the fact that there are certain circumstances under which it may lawfully be employed to excuse such action. Thus, for example, since the close of the eighteenth century, France, Germany, Austria, Italy, Spain, Belgium and Switzerland have declared that the principle of self-defense excused the action of a state in providing for the punishment of offenses of a serious nature committed beyond its borders, especially if such offenses were concerned with the counterfeiting of its currency, plotting against its ruler, or seeking to overthrow its existing government. Russia, Greece and Mexico have gone even further and declared that circumstances of exceptional necessity will excuse the action of a state in providing for the punishment of serious extraterritorial offenses against their subjects. It is understood, of course, that the enforcement of these laws shall take place within the limits of their respective sovereignties. That circumstances of exceptional necessity will excuse the passage of these laws appears also to be the opinion of the Institute of International Law. It has declared that: — " Every state has the right to punish acts committed even out of its territory, and by foreigners, in violation of its penal laws when these acts attack the social existence of the state in question and endanger its security, and are not provided against by the law of the country or the territory in which they have taken place." [102] It is believed that this statement represents a correct analysis of the situation its portrays.

In making a brief summary of necessity in its relation to the national jurisdiction, it may be pointed out that most of the cases in which the plea of necessity has been raised fall into two classes: — those in which the action is taken without regard to the law on the plea of necessity; and those in which no rule of law is in dispute but exceptional measures have been taken to enforce the law. In the first group of cases it is clear that the plea of necessity should be rejected; in the second group it may or may not be accepted, depending upon the circumstances of the case. It is doubtful if further classifications can be made with any degree of certainty. There are, however, two more groupings that may be tentatively presented: — A distinction may perhaps be made between certain acts which for want of a better name may be called acts of *passive* self-defense, such as the expulsion of aliens and laws against counterfeiting, in which the execution of the law takes place largely within the national jurisdiction, and *active* self-defense as illustrated by the pursuit of marauders across the borders of a neighboring country. The legal right to exercise such exceptional measures is clear in both cases; but it may with reason be argued that a greater degree of care in establishing the facts should be exercised in the second situation because it involves a violation of the law of territorial inviolability. A similar distinction may perhaps be made between those problems which have arisen so frequently in the past that the facts are well recognized as establishing necessity and those infrequent cases that involve the violation of a national jurisdiction. In both instances the facts must be established, but to illustrate the point it may be said that it is doubtless true that greater care should be exercised in establishing the fact of necessity in the cases involving the pursuit of hostile marauders by an armed troop than in the case of a peaceful merchant vessel making an involuntary entrance to a port.

III

NECESSITY AND THE HIGH SEAS

In dealing with the problem of necessity in its relation to the high seas it may be said that circumstances of exceptional necessity have been held to impose certain limitations upon the freedom of the seas in time of peace. It is in most cases a belligerent right to be exercised only in time of war; nevertheless such cases as *The Marianna Flora*[103] and *The Virginius*[104] may be cited in proof of the statement that the plea of necessity may be employed to excuse the act of visit and search in time of peace in the case of vessels which are reasonably believed to be engaged in an attempt to infringe the sovereignty or safety of the state making the search. Thus Mr. Cass, the American Secretary of State, in a note to Mr. Osma, the Peruvian minister, declared that: — " there is no case in which such entry [visit and search upon the high seas in time of peace] is a lawful act. It may be an excusable one under peculiar circumstances, of entrance and conduct, which might well induce the aggrieved party to renounce all claim for reparation, as, for instance, if a piratical vessel were known to be cruising in certain latitudes, and a national ship should fall in with a vessel sailing in those regions, and answering the description given of the pirate, the visitation of a peaceable merchantman in such a case, with a view to ascertaining her true character, would give no reasonable cause of offense to the nation to which she might belong, and whose flag she carried."[105] It is well established, however, that the danger must be serious and imminent and any other method of prevention must be impossible. Permission should also be limited to such action as is barely necessary for the purpose of self-preservation. Thus the power of the state making the visit and search would appear to be limited to keeping the ship and crew in custody as long as may be necessary for its safety and then in handing them over to their own state for trial and punishment. The plea of necessity, therefore, might lawfully have been employed to excuse the action of Spain in making a visit, search and detention of *The Virginius;* but it is doubtful if it would excuse her subsequent action in instituting proceedings against the crew; and it certainly would not excuse their court martial and execution as pirates.[106]

The plea of exceptional necessity as an excuse for visit and search was also advanced in connection with the efforts of certain states to suppress the slave trade. By Article VIII of the Webster-Ashburton Treaty of August 9, 1842, between the United States and Great Britain, the contracting parties agreed each to maintain on the African coast a sufficient squadron "to enforce, separately and respectively," their laws and obligations for the suppression of the slave trade. The two squadrons were to be "independent" of each other, but the two Governments were to give such instructions as would enable their forces effectually to act in concert and co-operation.[107] Subsequently a controversy arose between Great Britain and the United States as to whether a right of visit, as distinct from a right of visit and capture, could be exercised by the public ships of one state over private vessels flying the flag of the other, in order to ascertain if the claims of the flag were genuine. Such a right was asserted by Great Britain and denied by the United States. The United States, on the other hand, while refusing to admit that such a right existed, did nevertheless concede that circumstances of exceptional necessity might make such action the subject of excuse. Mr. Cass, in a note to Mr. Dallas, the American minister to Great Britain, declared that: ". . . they [the United States] concede that if, in the honest examination of a vessel sailing under American colors but accompanied by strongly marked suspicious circumstances, a mistake is made, and she is found to be entitled to the flag she bears, but no injury is committed and the conduct of the boarding party is irreproachable, no government would be likely to make a case thus exceptional in its character a subject of serious reclamation. . . ."[108] In the treaty of April 7, 1862, the United States abandoned its position and agreed to submit to the visit and search of its merchant vessels which upon reasonable grounds might be suspected of engaging in the African slave trade.[109]

It will be observed that while the similar plea of exceptional necessity is advanced, the situation involved in the suppression of the slave trade is essentially different from the one that arose in connection with *The Virginius*. In the first case it was alleged by Great Britain that such action was essential to carry out the object of a treaty and should be limited to such an examination of the vessel as would be barely necessary to ascertain her true character; in the case of *The Virginius* no treaty rights were involved and the circumstances of necessity were so exceptional in their nature that, as we have already stated, it is believed that Spain was justified in a detention of the vessel, although not, of course, in the trial and execution of the crew as pirates.

The plea of necessity has also been raised in connection with certain acts of piratical aggression upon the high seas. Thus it has been held that necessity will excuse the honest mistake of a state in attacking a ship that is conducting itself in a manner that would appear to indicate that it is a pirate *jure gentium*, even if it shall appear that such was not in fact the case.[110] A similar situation prevails in regard to the general problem of self-defense upon the high seas. It will confer upon a state, if its safety is threatened, a self-protective jurisdiction which will enable it, under circumstances of grave danger and suspicion, to visit upon the high seas a ship flying the flag of a foreign state, for the purpose of ascertaining her true object and destination, and it will also excuse the action of the visiting ship, if the evidence should warrant such a step, in taking charge of the ship and sending her in for adjudication. This was the situation in the case of *The Virginius*. A similar situation prevailed in the case of *The Mary Lowell*. She was, it is true, arrested within the territorial waters of a third state, but she was about to cross the high seas for the purpose of aiding insurgent members of the state making the arrest. In passing upon the validity of an international claim that arose in connection with the case, the umpire, Baron Blanc, declared that: — " the claimants forfeited their right to the protection of the American flag, and are estopped from asserting any of the privileges of lawful intercourse in times of peace and any title to individual benefit of indemnity as against the acts of the Spanish authorities done in self-defense."[111]

The danger, however, must be imminent in the sense that there must be reasonable proximity to the threatened territory and the conduct of the vessel must be such as to arouse grave suspicion. In such a case, moreover, notification should at once be made to the flag state, and those on board the arrested vessel should be placed at its disposal with a view to their punishment under their own municipal law.[112] This is due to the fact that the jurisdiction in such a case is merely protective and not punitive. If, on the other hand, the suspicion should prove unfounded, then an apology and indemnity should be offered; for in such a case the arresting state must be deemed to act at its peril.[113]

IV

NECESSITY AND THE PACIFIC INTERCOURSE OF STATES

THE problem of exceptional necessity in its relation to matters associated with the pacific intercourse of states has arisen chiefly in connection with aliens, jurisdictional immunities, and international claims.

The normal operation of the law requires that the alien about to be expelled should be notified of the charges against him and be given an opportunity to refute them. But circumstances of exceptional necessity, especially when the crime is of a political nature, will excuse an expulsion without a judicial conviction.[114] In such a case, however, the expelling government must be able to furnish proof that such a condition of exceptional necessity in fact existed. In the words of Mr. Gresham, the American Secretary of State, in protesting against the summary expulsion of the American citizen, Werner, by the Government of Haiti: —" If the case is so urgent and the presence of the foreigner so dangerous to the state that this [notice and hearing] cannot with safety be done, the expelling government is under obligation to the government of the person expelled to explain the grounds of its action, by not only presenting, but proving the existence of facts sufficient to justify the expulsion." [115] If it can be established that such a condition of exceptional necessity did not in fact exist to the extent of furnishing an excuse for the summary action taken, then an action may lie for an international claim and such claims have been considered by international commissions as just grounds for awards.[116]

It is, however, well established that military necessity will excuse the expulsion of aliens with a degree of suddenness and harshness that would not ordinarily be the subject of excuse in time of peace.[117] Thus the Institute has declared that: — " Military necessity will excuse the expulsion of aliens who in time of war or imminence of war compromise by their conduct the security of the state." [118] Such, indeed, has been the practice of states. In 1870 the French Government of National Defense expelled German subjects from the Department of the Seine as a measure of precaution in the presence of a grave military emergency; [119] and a similar argument was employed to excuse the expulsion of British subjects from South Africa at the outbreak of the Boer War,[120] Japanese subjects from Russian territory in the Far East at the outbreak of the Russo-Japanese War,[121] and certain classes of Italians from Turkey at the outbreak of the Italo-Turkish War in 1912.[122]

The problem of necessity has also arisen in connection with the extent to which it will excuse the placing of limitations upon the law of jurisdictional immunity. Thus, for example, exceptional necessity will excuse the action of the state to which a diplomatic mission is credited in imposing such a measure of restraint upon the action and conduct of the members of the mission as it shall feel is essential for its safety. Exceptional necessity will thus excuse the action of the territorial jurisdiction in placing the members of the diplomatic mission under temporary restraint and in this way preventing them from doing further harm.[123] Exceptional necessity will also excuse the action of a state to which a diplomatic agent is accredited in using force to restrain him from repeated violations of those commands and injunctions of the local police which do not restrain him in the effective exercise of his duties and which are of importance for the general order and safety of the community.[124] In the words of Mr. Moore: — " He may not, of course, be punished for his violation of these regulations but the state may, if it deem necessary, use force to restrain him from continued or repeated violations. . . . The immunity from judicial process cannot be perverted into a license to disregard the health and safety of the public, nor can it be construed as precluding the actual prevention of injuries to person or property, where, but for the exercise of immediate restraint, irreparable damage is threatened." [125]

Military necessity may also impose limitations upon the jurisdictional immunity of diplomatic agents that would not ordinarily be permitted in time of peace. Thus, for example, in time of war the diplomatic agent should take pains to see that in the exercise of his duties and especially in his exercise of the right of correspondence, he is not unwittingly opening a forbidden channel of communications to others than the persons addressed, which others may perhaps include the enemies of the country to which he is accredited. This was the charge made by Bismarck against certain foreign ambassadors in Paris during the siege of 1870, and the weight of evidence bears out his contention that he was justified on the ground of military necessity in imposing limitations upon the official correspondence of the diplomatic agents of neutral countries.[126]

The plea of exceptional necessity has also been employed to excuse the abrogation of a treaty and states have at times pleaded that circumstances of self-preservation and military necessity were of such a nature as to excuse them from an active fulfillment of the treaty obligation. This, for example, was one of the pleas advanced by Russia in 1871 to excuse her violation of the Treaty of Paris, and one of the pleas advanced by Germany in 1914 to excuse her violation of Belgium. This view has also received a certain amount of support from the publicists. Thus Hall declares that: — "A treaty . . . becomes voidable as soon as it is dangerous to the life or incompatible with the independence of a state, provided that its injurious effects were not intended by the two contracting parties at the time of its conclusion. Thus if the execution of a treaty of alliance or guarantee were demanded at a time when the ally or guaranteeing state were engaged in a struggle for its own existence or under circumstances which rendered war inevitable with another state against which success would be impossible, the country upon which the demand was made would be at liberty to decline to fulfill its obligations of alliance or guarantee."[127] Oppenheim also declares that when "the existence or the necessary development of a state stands in unavoidable conflict with such state's treaty obligations, the latter must give way, for self-preservation and development in accordance with the growth and necessary requirements of the nation are the primary duties of every state."[128] It is believed, however, that these writers have failed to distinguish carefully between self-preservation as a *sovereign* right and self-preservation as a right recognized in *international law.* Both Russia and Germany, in the cases cited above, were compelled by other states to repudiate their violations and it is not believed that the plea of necessity has been recognized in international law as a plea that will excuse the refusal to perform an international obligation enjoined by a treaty. It is not denied, however, that such an act may be justified as a sovereign right, nor is it believed that the refusal of international law to recognize the existence of such an international right, will exert any appreciable check upon the tendencies of states to repudiate their international obligations when they conceive that such action is essential for the protection of their sovereignty. But the weight of precedent and authority points to the fact that there is no warrant in international law to excuse such a violation on the plea of necessity.

The plea of necessity has frequently been employed to absolve a belligerent from responsibility for the payment of international claims and the plea of military necessity has been employed to excuse the payment of compensation due to private individuals for injuries to their persons or property resulting from legitimate acts of war, or the incidental and consequential results of a state of war. It will be more logical, however, to consider this topic in connection with necessity in its relation to war.

V

NECESSITY AND NON-AMICABLE MODES OF REDRESS SHORT OF WAR

THE problem of necessity has also been raised in relation to non-amicable modes of redress short of war. As a general principle of substantive law it may be said that the mode of redress employed has been one of intervention; but as a matter of procedure, the intervention has taken the various forms that will be discussed in this chapter.

The general problem of intervention is almost wholly a question of policy and not of law. In practically all the cases in which the plea of necessity has been employed to excuse an act of intervention, it has been insufficient to constitute a lawful excuse. Such a plea, however, appears at times to have the support of some of the most eminent authorities in international law; and they fail clearly to indicate the distinction that should be maintained between a legal and a political excuse. Thus Westlake has even gone so far as to maintain that circumstances of exceptional necessity will excuse the action of a state in intervening to protect itself in the innocent development of its power and influence, that is, the power and influence that is the natural outcome of its own strength, and not the result of depriving other states of their just political and territorial rights.[129] It is clear, however, that such an intervention cannot be excused on the ground of lawful necessity unless there has been a direct and open violation of sovereignty, such, for example, as an invasion of territory, and the state is unable to defend itself in any other way. This situation, as distinguished from a normal right of self-defense against attack, has already been discussed in connection with necessity and the national jurisdiction;[130] and, more particularly, it was considered in connection with the Florida invasions and the Caroline Affair.[131] The case cited by Westlake is essentially a political situation that has not yet been subject to regulation by the rules of international law simply because states have been unwilling to take such a step; and the precedents containing instances of international agreement upon the point under discussion are too fragmentary and incomplete for the framing of rules of international validity. The plea of necessity could not, therefore, be employed in legal justification and excuse.

It has also been said that circumstances of necessity will excuse the action of a state in intervening in the domestic affairs of another state when its own safety is endangered by conditions in the state against which the action is taken. It has even been held that necessity will excuse the action of a state in intervening to preserve the rights of succession of a certain ruler, if obligations due the intervening state were by treaty or agreement contingent upon his selection;[132] and intervention to maintain the balance of power when it can be established that any serious disruption of this balance constitutes a serious danger to the peace and security of the intervening state, or any group of intervening states.[133] Here again, however, the necessity referred to in these cases has not yet been made the subject of definite regulation by the rules of international law, and it is for this reason alone, if for no other, a type of political necessity.

In recent years the problem of intervention to maintain the balance of power has not infrequently been associated with certain policies of regional control and the alleged necessities of national defense. It has, for example, sometimes been maintained that a state may exert a certain measure of control over a weaker and less civilized neighbor, if such conduct is absolutely essential in order to defend the intervening state against the contingency of an attack arising out of the disturbed condition of affairs in the state against which the action is taken. Thus in the case of the Monroe Doctrine, the United States has defended its acts not only upon the ground of expediency, but has also at times maintained that circumstances of necessity have required that it assume a certain degree of responsibility for the condition of governments in Latin America, in order to defend itself against the possible contingency of a foreign intervention in those states which would in turn be dangerous to its own safety.[134] Since the announcement of the Monroe Doctrine, the United States has made such a plea in connection with the affairs of Mexico in 1861–65,[135] the northern frontier of the United States in 1867,[136] Cuba,[137] and also the Caribbean[138] and Lower California.[139]

It has been argued that an act of intervention under such circumstances is similar to the action of a state in taking steps to defend its natural jurisdiction against a dangerous external agency. Thus it has been said that American intervention in Cuba in 1898 may be excused on the ground that conditions prevailing there were dangerous to the safety of the people of the United States.[140] The writer does not deny that if the action of the state in intervening is clearly essential for the preservation of its own existence, it may be the subject of justification and excuse;[141] but such necessity ought to be established with the utmost definiteness. The danger ought to be of such a nature as seriously to threaten the existence of the state, and so imminent that other means of defense are lacking. The writer refers, in other words, to such a situation as prevailed in the case of the Florida invasions and the Caroline Affair.[142] Judged by these standards, it is believed that a legal justification for the type of intervention under discussion is rarely, if ever, to be found; and the writer cannot be too emphatic in giving his opinion to the effect that the cases of intervention that have been discussed in this chapter are political in their nature, and are not to be considered as subject to legal justification and excuse.

It has also been said that circumstances of exceptional necessity will excuse the action of a state in intervening to protect the lives and property of its citizens from a serious danger that may threaten their existence; and that such an intervention may be made the subject of excuse if there has been in the state against which the intervention is directed, an absence or failure of administrative authority.[143] It is believed, however, that in practically all the cases in which the plea has been raised as a lawful excuse for the protection of lives and property of aliens, it will be found that we are confronted with another aspect of political intervention. So far as an alien is concerned, it is difficult to see how his state would have a lawful right to send troops merely because his license to trade had been revoked, or even because his property had been confiscated, provided such acts had been carried out in accordance with the laws of the state, or in accordance with the needs of its police power, and there has been no discrimination against the aliens of a particular state. We do not, of course, deny that such acts may be carried out in a manner that will justify a diplomatic interposition; but an intervention in the form of landing troops will be the subject of legal excuse only in case that refraining from such action would result in a most vital breach in the sovereign rights of the state affected. Intervention would perhaps be the subject of legal excuse if the lives of a large number of aliens were in imminent danger, and there had been clear evidence that the state in which they resided was unable or unwilling to protect them. Thus the plea of necessity might lawfully be employed to excuse the intervention of the Great Powers in China at the time of the Boxer Rebellion; but it is one of the few cases that can be clearly established. Such outbreaks as the Boxer trouble are rare in modern times, and would appear to be confined to portions of the world where there is an absence of constituted authority, as appears to have been the situation in the Greytown case;[144] or in semi-civilized states suffering from a temporary relapse into barbarism and placing the lives of a large number of aliens in imminent danger. This was the situation which appears to have characterized the Boxer outbreak.

The argument against the employment of the plea of necessity as a lawful excuse for intervention by the use of force is even stronger in the case of its use for the protection of property situated in foreign countries. This question has become more important in recent years because of the increase in the amount of investments of foreign capital, and the rules of international law have failed to keep pace with this development. With the law in its present state, however, we can say that the plea of necessity ought not to be employed to excuse an intervention by the use of force in behalf of property rights alone, unless there has been a loss of property so vital in its nature and so vast in its scope as seriously to threaten the sovereignty of the state involved, and carried out in such a way as to show that it has been accompanied with a serious disregard for private law, or with clear intent to discriminate against the aliens of a particular state. Even then it is to be doubted that such an intervention in behalf of property rights may be made the subject of legal excuse unless the injured state has first exhausted all means at its disposal in attempting to make a settlement by diplomacy or arbitration of the points in dispute. Judged by these standards, the writer is unable to recall a single instance in modern times in which it can be clearly established that the plea of necessity has been lawfully employed to excuse an act of intervention solely in behalf of property rights. As the law exists at present, it would appear that practically the only cases in which it should be made the subject of a legal excuse are cases of defense against sudden invasion, such as the Florida and Caroline incidents, where the circumstances are so exceptional in their nature as to set them apart from normal cases of self-defense exercised against an invasion by a foreign power; and such cases as the Boxer Rebellion and, perhaps, Greytown, in which there is a complete absence or breakdown of sovereign authority, resulting in the most imminent danger to the lives and property of a large class of aliens belonging to the intervening state. Greytown was also a community that claimed the right to exist outside the limits of any recognized national jurisdiction.

The plea of necessity has also been employed to excuse the action of a state in resorting to non-amicable modes of redress in the form of the use of force, pacific blockade, and reprisals. The use of force by the authorities of a state may constitute the exercise of a normal right and not an exceptional measure of self-defense; but the plea of exceptional self-defense has been employed to excuse the action of the agents of a state in using force under certain exceptional circumstances and without special authority. Thus, as we have already seen, the plea of exceptional necessity was employed by the United States to excuse the action of a commander of one of its warships, who, in 1854, bombarded Greytown, Nicaragua, and destroyed it by fire, after the authorities had failed to grant the redress demanded. President Pierce, in seeking to prove that circumstances of exceptional necessity constituted an excuse for the action of the American commander, declared that Greytown " was, in fact, a marauding establishment too dangerous to be disregarded and too guilty to pass unpunished, and yet incapable of being treated in any other way than as a piratical resort of outlaws or a camp of savages depredating on emigrant trains or caravans and the frontier settlements of civilized states." [145] It should be observed that even this case was not devoid of certain political considerations involving a struggle between Great Britain and the United States for the control of territory in Nicaragua; [146] but at the same time the weight of evidence would appear to point to the fact that the plea of necessity advanced by the United States was subject to a legal justification and excuse. Thus, in refusing to pay the claims of French subjects for alleged loss of property sustained in the Greytown bombardment, Secretary of State Marcy declared that " . . . if the subjects or citizens of foreign states choose to become dwellers among such an assemblage, and entrust their property to such a custody, they can have no just cause to complain, nor good grounds for the redress of injuries resulting from the punishment inflicted upon the offending community." [147] He also pointed out that these foreigners had refused an offer of protection prior to the bombardment, and he added: — " As they did not claim it when it might have been advisable, they cannot, in good grace, do so now, to sustain extravagant demands for their losses." [148] Lord Palmerston refused to present claims for losses sustained by British subjects in the bombardment; and it is significant that he admitted the legality of the action of the United States in carrying out the bombardment. He specifically refers to " the right which the law of nations gave them to take measures which they, in their own judgment, deemed necessary." [149] It is clear, then, that the Greytown case received a legal justification at the hands of the state authorities. At the same time the question may be raised as to whether the facts were of such a nature as to warrant it. The measures taken by Captain Hollins, the American commander, were professedly in pursuance of general instructions to obtain reparation for the losses sustained by the Accessory Transit Company, an organization of American citizens, and for an indignity that had been suffered by Mr. Borland, an American minister to Central America; and while it is true that his government later upheld the specific measures taken by Captain Hollins upon his own initiative, it would seem to the present writer that his conduct in the bombardment and burning of Greytown was ruthless and in excess of the actual necessities of the case. It is true that Greytown was an unorganized and irresponsible community, but it may be questioned whether President Pierce was justified in comparing the wrongs that had been committed by the people of Greytown with the depredations of savages upon emigrant trains and frontier settlements.[150] The plea of exceptional necessity was also advanced by President McKinley to excuse the use of force without Congressional authority in the case of the American Relief Expedition to Peking in 1900.[151] It is clear, however, that it will require a situation of the utmost gravity, and one that seriously threatens the impairment of vital national rights, together with the inability to make an appeal to a responsible and organized government, to excuse the exercise of such harsh measures as were employed in the affair at Greytown.

A pacific blockade would appear, in most cases to be the exercise of a normal and legitimate measure against the state or body of insurgents against whom it is directed.[152] The plea of exceptional necessity, on the other hand, has been employed to excuse its interference with the commerce of third powers, when such action is the result of a concert of certain states to enforce certain measures of international police in behalf of the sovereign of a semi-civilized state whose affairs constituted a menace to international order, and who has given consent to such action. It has been said that such a situation constitutes a case of exceptional necessity which will excuse the action of the powers instituting the blockade in turning away the ships of third states which are attempting to penetrate the blockade, or in detaining them until the objects for which the blockade was instituted have been attained. This was the attitude taken by the Great Powers in the blockade of Zanzibar in 1888–89, and in the blockade of Crete in 1897. The first case was an effort on the part of the Great Powers to suppress the slave trade and the importation of arms with the consent of the native ruler, and the interference with the ships of third states was limited strictly to the stoppage of those engaged in the import of munitions and the export of slaves. The second case was an effort on the part of the Great Powers, with the consent of the Sultan of Turkey, to restore order in Crete during the intervention of 1897; and in seeking to attain this object, there was a certain amount of interference with the ships of third states engaged in carrying munitions to the insurgents. The plea of exceptional necessity was employed to excuse the action taken, and it has been described as *un droit des gens special pour les besoins de la cause.*[153]

The extent to which the plea of necessity should be permitted to interfere with the trading rights of third states in cases of pacific blockade would appear to be extremely limited in its scope. States engaged in a pacific blockade may perhaps be permitted to employ it to excuse their violation of the less important trading rights of a third state, if such action is vitally essential to the maintenance of their own safety. The Cretan intervention of 1897 may perhaps be considered a case in point. It may have been essential to take such action in order to maintain the Concert of Europe in relation to the Near Eastern Question, and to prevent a grave international crisis. But states ought not to employ the plea of necessity for the purpose of excusing a serious interference with the trading rights of third states in defense of rights that are not vital, and cases of doubt ought always to be resolved in favor of third states, for the right of these states to engage in peaceful trade is paramount. Non-intervention with this trade is the rule — intervention by means of a peaceful blockade is an exception which circumstances of the utmost urgency will alone excuse. It should also be observed that in a comparatively recent case, the pacific blockade of Venezuela by Great Britain and Germany in 1902, the blockading powers conceded that they could not lawfully act against the vessels of the United States, a third and protesting state.[154]

The plea of necessity has also been employed at times in an effort to excuse the exercise of reprisals in time of peace. Thus England, in 1849, blockaded the ports of Greece and seized a number of Greek vessels in an attempt to gain satisfaction for a number of claims including the famous claim of Don Pacifico.[155] The British Government endeavored to defend its action by pointing to its " patience and forbearance . . . during so many years," together with " the numerous previous friendly expostulations . . . ; the very mild measures at first resorted to; the slow degrees by which coercive measures have been proceeded with; [and] the extreme reluctance with which recourse has at last been had to measures affecting Greek commerce. . . ."[156] In view of these conditions Great Britain finally declared: — " The continued refusal of the Greek Government to satisfy the demands made on it by that of Her Majesty for redressing the outrages and losses sustained by British and Ionian subjects [had] rendered it necessary to make reprisals of Greek merchant vessels. . . ."[157]

It is clear, however, that the plea of necessity, in its technical sense, should not be associated with reprisals. An act of reprisal may be considered the operation of a normal rule of law in all cases of international delinquency for which the injured state cannot get reparation through negotiation.[158] Thus Article I of Convention II of the Hague Rules of 1907, in dealing with the limitation of the employment of force for the recovery of contract debts, declares that reprisals by means of armed forces can only be resorted to in case the debtor state refuses to arbitrate,[159] and no mention is made of necessity as a plea in extenuation and excuse.

Not only is the weight of authority clearly against the employment of the plea of necessity in association with reprisal in time of peace, but it is also evident that such cases are clearly to be distinguished from those in which the plea of necessity is made, on the basis of the facts and conditions involved. It will be observed that the plea of necessity has been employed in extenuation and excuse in connection with non-amicable modes of redress short of war in such cases as the Florida invasions and the Caroline Affair, where there has been a continuing danger, directed against the national domain, involving a serious danger to human life, and emanating from a source where there was an absence of governmental authority, or a governmental authority unable or unwilling to restrain such a dangerous agency. In the Boxer intervention of 1900, it is true that the dangerous agency was not directed against the national domains of the intervening states, but against foreign nationals domiciled in China; but the other three conditions prevailed, — there was a continuing danger, it involved a serious danger to human life, and the Chinese Government was unable or unwilling to prevent it. In the Greytown case, there was, as we have seen, a complete absence of responsible government. It cannot, however, be said that these facts existed in connection with the English intervention in Greece in 1849 — the Don Pacifico case — and they do not exist in the great majority of cases in which an intervention is made for the recovery of contract debts in general. One may agree with Hall that "there is not only no necessity, but as a rule the acts for which reprisals are made, except when reprisals are used as a mere introduction to war, are of comparative unimportance."[160] In such cases as that of Don Pacifico, and in those involving the recovery of contract debts in general, there is certainly no present and continuing danger, since the dispute largely involves the discussion of past events; there is no vital danger to sovereignty and the national domain, since the discussion involves the problem of contract and property rights in a foreign state; there is no danger to human life; and finally, recourse may be had to the courts of the foreign state. Perhaps the weakest point of England's plea in the case of Don Pacifico lies in the fact that the demands upon the Greek Government were made before she had exhausted her legal remedies in the Greek courts.[161]

VI

MILITARY NECESSITY

In dealing with the problem of military necessity, it is the purpose of the writer to discuss the general relation of the idea of necessity to a state of war; the extent to which the specific doctrine of necessity may lawfully be employed to excuse a departure from the more or less generally recognized rules of warfare; and, finally, the extent to which the rules of law may be said to impose limitations upon the practice of acts of military necessity.

A state of war itself may be said to constitute an exceptional condition in the sense that it marks a radical departure from the normal rules of international intercourse that tend to prevail in time of peace. The old aphorism, *inter arma silent leges,* still contains a certain amount of truth if it is employed to describe the effect of war upon the laws of peace. But the modern science of international law has developed a certain body of rules and regulations which, while subject to differences of interpretation at many points, and not infrequently vague, indefinite and incomplete, may nevertheless be referred to with considerable exactness as the rules of warfare. That these rules are not always clear and comprehensive, and that they are subject to modification and change, should not be unduly emphasized. The same situation tends also to prevail in private law, and it is safe to say that in certain cases the rules of warfare have been as definitely ascertained and are as generally observed as are some of the rules and statutes of public law. Thus, for example, the rule of law that there shall be no slaughter of helpless prisoners of war is certainly more consistently observed than is the recent 18th Amendment of the Constitution of the United States. It is undoubtedly true that the definite and clearly established rules of warfare are comparatively few in number and of considerable less complexity than the laws of peace which they tend to supersede. They have as their chief object an attempt to mitigate some of the rigors of war and to protect the rights of non-combatants and neutrals. It is the purpose of the writer to endeavor to ascertain the extent to which the rules of warfare which have been more or less definitely recognized as possessing legality may be lawfully modified by the plea of military necessity. One theory of military necessity has endeavored to emphasize the fact that there are certain rules of international warfare so firmly established that no employment of the doctrine of necessity will excuse their violation unless the rule itself contains a more or less definite statement of the circumstances under which violations by reason of this plea will be excused. This theory holds, in other words, that the doctrine of necessity should be limited to those circumstances in which the law has in advance given an express sanction for its use. This, in general, appears to be the view of military necessity that has been held by the leading authorities of the United States and England.[162]

The other theory of military necessity is expressed by the aphorism, *Kriegsraison geht vor Kriegsmanier* — military expediency overrules the manner of warfare. This theory has perhaps been advanced by German writers of international law to a greater extent than by those of any other country, and appears to mean that while ordinarily the rules of warfare should be respected, they ought nevertheless to impose no limitations upon the ultimate safety of the state, and therefore circumstances of vital necessity should excuse their violation.[163] This was essentially the plea advanced by Germany to justify the devastations of the Somme region during the retreat in the spring of 1917 and the general retreat in the autumn of 1918.[164]

Of these two views, the writer subscribes to the first, as the only one that is legally valid: — that the doctrine of necessity should be limited to those circumstances in which the law has in advance given an express sanction for its use. This statement of the rule has the advantage that it constitutes a legal minimum upon which all states may agree. The German theory has been wholly denied by other states; but German publicists would subscribe to the definition above as correct as far as it goes. But aside from the fact that other states did not agree with the German theory, it is, for other reasons, clearly untenable. It is not a legal method of procedure for a vitally interested party to be able to change the rules of warfare at a moment's notice upon a plea of necessity; it reduces international law from a controlling to a registering agency; [165] and it would appear to be a clear violation of the spirit and letter of the Hague Rules. In the preamble to the convention to which the rules are annexed, the High Contracting Parties state that in the provisions which they have adopted " the wording . . . has been inspired by the desire to diminish the evils of war as far as military necessities permit, [and] are intended to serve as a general rule of conduct for belligerents in their relations with each other and with populations." [166] If this statement is considered together with the fact that a number of these conventional rules regulating warfare are actually qualified with references to military necessity,[167] and the additional fact that Article XXII of the Hague Rules distinctly states that the right of belligerents to adopt means of injuring the enemy is not unlimited, and that this rule does not lose its binding force in a case of necessity, it would appear to point unquestionably to the conclusion that the framers of the Hague Rules intended to limit the lawful exercise of necessity to those cases in which they had granted an express sanction for its use.[168]

The problem of the extent to which the plea of military necessity may lawfully be employed to excuse a departure from the rules of war, may be considered first, in connection with military operations themselves; and secondly, in connection with matters that are not so directly concerned with military operations.

In the first group of cases the plea of military necessity has been raised chiefly in connection with belligerent forces, belligerent measures and instrumentalities, the grant of quarter, the treatment of prisoners of war, the sick and the wounded.

The present rules of military necessity in their relation to the qualifications of belligerents have been established as the logical result of conditions which have had as their object the separation of the military and non-military groups of the belligerent state into two distinct classes. Various conferences have discussed the problem, and attempts to define the nature of a belligerent organization were undertaken by the Declaration of Brussels in 1874, the Institute of International Law in its meeting at The Hague in 1875, and the Hague Conference of 1899. These conferences developed the fact that the large and small states entertained different conceptions of their military necessities in relation to this question of belligerent organization, — the large states insisting upon strict organization and control, and the smaller states pointing out that they must rely upon informal uprisings of their people in order to defend themselves against invaders. It is true that Article II of the Hague Conference of 1899 declared that: — " The inhabitants of a territory which has not been occupied who, on the approach of the enemy, spontaneously take up arms to resist the invading troops without having had time to organize themselves in accordance with Article I,[169] shall be regarded as belligerents if they carry arms openly and if they respect the laws and customs of war." [170] But during the World War Germany was able to point out that Article II of the Hague Regulations of 1899 was not technically binding upon her and she then proceeded to urge that military necessity compelled her to deal with levies *en masse* as she had treated them in 1870–71 — that is, to hold that such levies should be organized in the same manner as volunteer troops and should wear distinctive marks visible at a distance.[171] This interpretation of military necessity led her to treat with great severity all acts of hostility which were not subject to these regulations. Such unauthorized firing upon German troops was punished by the execution of the offenders, the burning of houses, the execution of hostages taken from among the older and more important personages of the district, and the employment of civilians as fire screens in posts of danger.[172] In all of these cases Germany insisted that the unorganized nature of the attack compelled her to adopt these measures of exceptional severity. The Belgian Government did not altogether deny the German charges but in extenuation pleaded its inability wholly to control the acts of irresponsible individuals. On the basis of customary law the German plea of military necessity would appear to possess a large measure of validity. The degree of force employed should have been no greater than was necessary to protect the army of occupation, — but this is a question of fact to be determined in future years by the historian of the German occupation. It has been pointed out that Article L of the Hague Regulations declared that: — "No general penalty, pecuniary or otherwise, shall be inflicted upon the population on account of the acts of individuals for which they cannot be regarded as jointly and severally responsible." [173]

Military necessity in its relation to belligerent measures and instrumentalities would appear to excuse the use of military measures which contain a certain amount of exceptional harshness. Thus it has been held that if a town, even though undefended, puts up an active resistance, it may be bombarded; and so, too, if it is occupied by the enemy. These circumstances might, indeed, be said to constitute a part of the normal law of war; but exceptional circumstances of military necessity may also excuse the bombardment of such a town if it is of value to the enemy in connection with a definite military objective,—if, for example, it served to obstruct a line of attack, or if it served to provide a shelter to which the enemy might retire. In such a situation it is doubtless true that "the attacker could justify a bombardment of it under plea of military necessity; it is practically included in the perimeter of defense and may be considered as co-operating with the fortress." [174]

In addition to those bombardments which are the direct result of military operations, military necessity will also excuse the occupation of undefended cities for the purpose of destroying general military supplies, or securing compliance with legitimate requisitions, or inflicting punishment by way of reprisals for infractions of the laws of war on the part of the enemy.[175] Thus Article XXV of the Hague Rules of 1907 in forbidding the bombardment of undefended towns,[176] does not mean that such towns may not be destroyed as a measure of military necessity.

Article XXVI of the Hague Rules of 1907 declares that: —"The officer in command of an attacking force must, before commanding a bombardment, except in cases of assault, do all in his power to warn the authorities." [177] Thus the military necessities of a surprise attack may excuse a commander in failing to do this.[178]

It is doubtful if military necessity will excuse the bombardment of non-combatants in order to produce psychological pressure upon the combatants and thus induce them to surrender. But even as in the case of the undefended town, and with even more logic and reason, military necessity will excuse the destruction of all life and property within the invested area which occurs as the inevitable result of military operations directed against the defenders. Thus in siege operations as conducted prior to the World War, it not infrequently happened that the defenses were built so close to the town that the latter received a shelling. General Sherman defended his shelling of Atlanta by replying to General Hood: — "you defended Atlanta on a line so close to town that every cannon-shot and many musket-shot from our line of investment that shot over their mark, went into the habitations of women and children." [179]

Hospitals and public buildings and monuments should be spared; but on the other hand, military necessity also requires that these objects must not be so numerous or located in such a way as to interfere with the prosecution of lawful military operations. Thus in the Russo-Turkish War, the Turks complained that the Russian gunners shelled the hospitals in Rustchuck, but von Martens points out that this was quite unavoidable because: — "They had organized some hospitals flying the Red Crescent in the center of the town, so that, to spare the privileged places, the Russians would have had to renounce every act of hostility." [180] A similar situation arose during the Russo-Japanese War. It may be pointed out, therefore, that a correct interpretation of military necessity in its relation to the bombardment of hospitals was doubtless made by the Japanese at the siege of Port Arthur in the following statement: —

1. " . . . the Japanese Army does not under any circumstances range its artillery intentionally against hospitals displaying the sign of the Red Cross, but as the buildings marked on the plan as hospitals are situated in the midst of, or quite close to, those which we deem it essential to bombard, we cannot be absolutely certain that the shells will not touch them by accident owing to the deviation of our ordnance."

2. " As declared by the delegate of our army in the negotiation of the 16th inst., the fact of our receiving the plan does not imply our acceptance of the obligation of not firing intentionally upon the buildings marked as hospitals. We reserve the right to range our guns on such of these buildings . . . if we learn . . . that there is a violation of the Geneva Convention with regard to a particular building, although it is being actually used as a hospital." [181]

The Hague Rules also provide for the immunity of " buildings dedicated to religion, art, science, or charitable purposes," [182] — subject, of course, to the principle that military necessity, if not the normal rules of war, will justify their destruction, if in any way they are occupied or used for warlike purposes.

The development of warfare during the World War would appear to call for a reconsideration of the whole question of necessity in its relation to sieges and bombardments. As examples of military necessity in its relation to new methods of warfare, may be cited the use of long-range guns, which made it impossible to distinguish public buildings; the question of whether the massing and entraining of large bodies of troops in such congested areas as London and Paris made them " defended towns "; and, most important of all, the difficulty of regulating bombardments made by airplanes traveling at great height and speed. It has been pointed out that the increasing use of the airplane has made it almost impossible any longer to maintain the " defense " test in regard to the bombardment of towns. It is now possible for an air fleet to travel from a distant aerodrome and defend from the air a town which is wholly undefended so far as ground defense are concerned.[183] It has therefore been suggested that military necessity should excuse the bombing of all active war zones; and that the actual existence of such a zone is to be determined by a consideration of whether the military elements in the given area are more vital than the non-military. If this attitude were adopted, it is possible that the plea of military necessity would be employed to excuse the wholesale destruction of all kinds of property susceptible of military use by bombardment from the air. It is, however, the contention of Spaight that international law " should refuse to countenance any departure from the principle that air-force necessity permits the destruction of non-military property only when non-combatants in the vicinity *have at least the opportunity to provide for their safety,* and that attack upon such property is absolutely banned when it must involve necessarily the sacrifice of innocent life."[184] He concludes, therefore, that: — " Air forces will seek bigger game — the kind of property the destruction of which must have an important repercussion on the whole fabric of national life and business. . . . Slowly, surely, inevitably, so far as we can see, war on property must replace war on life. The more effective will drive out the less effective method."[185] We are thus led to the somewhat paradoxical conclusion that military necessity may be compelled to respect the so-called rights of humanity, not because they are conceived to have any value, but because of their relative worthlessness and unimportance from a military point of view when compared with the greater military value attached to property that is susceptible of military use. Grim as this conclusion may appear to be, it is nevertheless very possible that even it may rest upon an insecure foundation of optimism and hope. Of what use is property unless there are people to direct its use? If some means could be found to exterminate whole populations by means of poison gases hurled from the air, would not the plea of military necessity be advanced to excuse the use of such a method as the surest means of exterminating the enemy, and at the same time of depriving him of the ability to employ his property in belligerent uses? As a matter of fact, there would appear to be no essential difference between an undefended town to which troops may have access and one which may be defended by air; and as the law stands at the present time, the only legal excuse for the bombardment of an undefended town is that it constitutes a vital military objective within the area of hostilities.

It was for the purpose of attempting to settle some of the problems that have arisen in connection with the use of aircraft in warfare that a commission of jurists met at The Hague in 1922–23. The commission proceeded to draft a code for the regulation of the use of aircraft and radio in time of war. It is important to note that considerable attention was devoted to the problem of military necessity in its relation to the aircraft of belligerent and neutral states. Thus the commission declared that: — "Aerial bombardment is legitimate only when directed at a military objective — that is to say, an object of which the destruction or injury would constitute a distinct military advantage to the belligerent."[186] It also declared that: — "In the immediate neighborhood of the operations of land forces, the bombardment of cities, towns, villages, dwellings or buildings is legitimate provided there exists a reasonable presumption that the military concentration is sufficiently important to justify such bombardment, having regard to the danger thus caused to the civilian population."[187] The problem of military necessity in relation to bombardment by belligerent aircraft is also regulated by Article XXV, which declares that: — "In bombardment by aircraft, all necessary steps must be taken by the commander to spare, as far as possible, buildings dedicated to public worship, art, science, or charitable purposes, historic monuments, hospital ships, hospitals and other places where the sick and wounded are collected, provided such buildings, objects or places are not at the time used for military purposes. Such buildings, objects and places must by day be indicated by marks visible to aircraft."[188]

The problem of military necessity is also considered in relation to "military authority over enemy and neutral aircraft and persons on board." The convention declared that: — "In case a belligerent commanding officer considers that the presence of aircraft is likely to prejudice the success of operations in which he is engaged at the moment, he may prohibit the passing of neutral aircraft in the immediate vicinity of his forces, or may oblige them to follow a particular route. A neutral aircraft which does not conform to such directions, of which it has had notice issued by the belligerent commanding officer, may be fired upon."[189] Article XXV also declares that: — "Neutral aircraft flying within the jurisdiction of a belligerent and warned of the approach of military aircraft of the opposing belligerent, must make the nearest available landing. Failure to do so exposes them to the risk of being fired upon."[190]

In the case of persons on board enemy military aircraft who fall into the hands of a belligerent and who cannot be made prisoners of war, Article XXXVI declares that: — "Release may . . . be delayed if the military interests of the belligerent so require."[191] Mr. Moore explains this article by stating that: — "The fact that military exigencies may necessitate temporary delay in according release does not prejudice the right to such release in due course." [192]

In dealing with the problem of "Belligerent Duties towards Neutral States and Neutral Duties towards Belligerent States," Article LVIII declares that: — "Private aircraft which are found upon visit and search to be neutral aircraft liable to condemnation upon the ground of unneutral service, or upon the ground that they have no external marks or are bearing false marks, may be destroyed, if sending them in for adjudication would be impossible or would imperil the safety of the belligerent aircraft or the success of the operations in which it is engaged. Apart from the causes mentioned above, a neutral private aircraft must not be destroyed except in the gravest military emergency which would not justify the officer in command in releasing it or sending it in for adjudication." [193] Neutral interests are further protected in Article LIX, which declares that "the persons on board must be placed in safety, the papers secured, and the captor must then bring the case before the prize court where he must establish the need for destruction and the validity of the capture. Failure to do this will expose the captor to the risk of paying compensation and making restitution." [194]

Finally, Article LX declares that: — "When a neutral private aircraft is captured on the ground that it is carrying contraband, the captor may demand the surrender of any absolute contraband on board, or may proceed to the destruction of such absolute contraband, if sending in the aircraft for adjudication is impossible or would imperil the safety of the belligerent aircraft or the success of the operations in which it is engaged. After entering in the log book of the aircraft the delivery or destruction of the goods, and securing, in original or copy, the relevant papers of the aircraft, the captor must allow the neutral aircraft to continue its flight." [195]

The Hague Rules state that it is especially forbidden to declare that no quarter will be given; [196] but there are doubtless times when the plea of military necessity may be employed to excuse the refusal of such a grant. It has been pointed out that it is sometimes impossible to grant quarter in savage warfare because barbarian tribesmen may lack sufficient intelligence or will properly to take advantage of it; and the grant may thus serve needlessly to expose the lives of the victors; [197] or in cases of fighting at close quarters, or in hot pursuit by cavalry, where it is difficult to single out those individuals who desire to surrender from the mass without undue delay to the accomplishment of the general objective — the capture of the hostile area and the complete defeat of the enemy.[198]

Military necessity in its relation to the treatment of actual prisoners of war was recognized by the Hague Rules in connection with the following provisions: — Article V declares that: — "Prisoners of war may be interned in a town, fortress, camp, or other place, and bound not to go beyond certain fixed limits; but they cannot be confined except as an indispensable measure of safety and only while the circumstances which necessitate the measure continue to exist." [199] Article VIII also declares that: — "Prisoners of war shall be subject to the laws, regulations, and orders in force in the army of the state in whose power they are. Any act of insubordination justifies the adoption towards them of such measures of severity as may be considered necessary." [200]

It therefore follows from an interpretation of Article V that circumstances of military necessity will justify a belligerent in placing its prisoners of war in confinement. During the Boer War, for example, Lord Roberts complained to

President Kruger of the South African Republic that British prisoners were confined as ordinary criminals. In extenuation and excuse President Kruger explained that certain prisoners who had committed offenses against the laws of war and were awaiting trial, and others who had attempted to escape, or were suspected of an intention to escape, had been confined in a common prison as a measure of safety, but were kept apart from the ordinary prisoners, and Lord Roberts appears to have accepted this explanation as satisfactory.[201]

The Hague Rules declare that: — "The obligations of belligerents with regard to the sick and wounded are governed by the Geneva Convention." [202] Article I of the Geneva Convention of 1906 deals more or less directly with the problem of military necessity in its relation to the sick and wounded when it declares that: — ". . . a belligerent who is compelled to abandon sick and wounded to the enemy shall, as far as military exigencies permit, leave with them a portion of his military personnel and material to contribute to the care of them." [203] Military necessity will, therefore, excuse the action of a belligerent who abandons his sick and wounded without leaving a sufficient medical personnel to care for their needs, if he is absolutely unable to make such provisions; and at the same time military necessity will excuse the action of the enemy in failing adequately to provide for them if he also is unable to do so. Thus in the Russo-Japanese War, the commander of the Japanese Army in Manchuria complained to the Russian commander that the latter was leaving so many wounded lying upon the battlefield that the Japanese medical corps was absolutely unable to handle the situation; and at the same time he requested the Russian commander to exercise more care in the removal of his sick and wounded.[204]

Military necessity may also excuse the action of a belligerent in his failure to collect the casualties after an engagement. Military necessity may sometimes require that a belligerent continue to sweep a position with shot and shell to prevent its occupation by the enemy; and under these circumstances the sick and wounded must lie untended.[205] Military necessity will also justify such action if the holders of a position cannot permit the searching parties of the enemy to approach lest they discover the secrets of their defenses.[206] Military necessity will also justify the action of a belligerent in refusing to grant a delay for such a purpose if he feels that he needs the time to strengthen his defenses.[207]

Article V of the Geneva Convention also states that: — "The competent military authority may appeal to the charitable zeal of the inhabitants to collect and take care of, under his direction, the wounded or sick of armies, granting to those who respond to the appeal special protection and certain immunities."[208] It is evident, however, that military necessity will justify the action of a commander in the requisition of public and private buildings for such a purpose.[209] Article VII declares that: — "The protection to which medical units and establishments are entitled ceases if they are made use of to commit acts harmful to the enemy";[210] and Article VIII declares that a medical unit does not lose its protection if "it uses its arms for its own defense or for that of the sick and wounded under its charge."[211] Article IX declares that: — "The personnel engaged exclusively in the collection, transport, and treatment of the wounded and the sick, as well as in the administration of medical units and establishments, and the chaplains attached to armies, shall be respected and protected under all circumstances. If they fall into the hands of the enemy they shall not be treated as prisoners of war."[212] This rule, however, is subject to the law of military necessity to the extent that if the military personnel is in danger of discovering vital military secrets, it may be warned to retire, and if it fails to do so, the exigencies of military defense may compel the belligerent to open fire.[213] Article XV declares that: — "The buildings and material of fixed establishments remain subject to the laws of war, but may not be diverted from their purpose so long as they are necessary for the wounded and the sick. Nevertheless the commander of troops in the field may dispose of them, in case of urgent military necessity, provided they make previous arrangements for the welfare of the wounded and sick who are found there." [214] Thus military necessity would doubtless excuse a belligerent in removing the patients from a hospital if the town were attacked, and such action were necessary in order to put it in a state of defense. Article XVII declares that: — "Convoys of evacuation shall be treated like mobile medical units " [215] subject to certain provisions. One of these provisions is that: — "A belligerent intercepting a convoy may break it up if military exigencies demand, provided he takes charge of the sick and wounded who are in it." [216]

In our second group of cases the problem of military necessity has been raised chiefly in connection with certain problems associated with the pacific intercourse of belligerents, the seizure, requisition, destruction, and devastation of enemy property and the treatment of non-combatants. This group of cases also constitutes one in which the exercise of necessity should be held within the strictest possible limits. It is more difficult in these cases to prove the existence of a vital military objective; and it is essential to respect such features as flags of truce, private property and the rights of non-combatants, in order to keep open the door for a cessation of warfare, and, in the meantime, to impose strict limits upon its rigors.

The plea of military necessity has been employed to excuse certain acts in relation to the pacific intercourse of belligerents and more especially certain acts in relation to flags of truce, cartels, suspensions of arms and truces and armistices. Thus military necessity will excuse the act of a belligerent commander in refusing to admit the bearer of a flag of truce while a secret movement is being executed, or in the midst of an engagement when "to suspend the fighting at the very moment the parlementaire presents himself, would be to risk sacrificing the victory at the decisive moment of paralyzing the pursuit." [217] Military necessity will also excuse the action of a commander in firing upon the bearer of a flag of truce, who, after being warned to retire, persists in advancing.[218] Military necessity will also excuse its disregard when it is hoisted not by a parlementaire who goes forward to meet the enemy in the recognized way but by a retreating force for the purpose of staying the hand of the enemy.[219] Military necessity will also excuse the action of a belligerent commander in refusing to grant a flag of truce for the purpose of removing the dead and wounded between the lines. Thus it will excuse the action of Lee in refusing such a request from Grant after Cold Harbor; [220] and the action of the Russian defenders of Port Arthur in turning their searchlights and guns on the fatigue parties sent by the Japanese to search for their wounded.[221]

Military necessity may also excuse the action of a belligerent in refusing, at least temporarily, to grant a suspension of arms, a truce or an armistice. Thus, as has already been indicated, military necessity may excuse the action of a belligerent commander in refusing to grant a suspension for the removal of the dead or wounded. During the siege of Port Arthur, for example, circumstances of military necessity compelled both sides to make such a refusal.[222] Military necessity will also excuse the act of a commander in refusing if he has reason to believe that the offer is made by the enemy for the purpose of aiding him in his military defense. Thus in the Boer War, Lord Roberts refused to accede to Cronje's request for an armistice at Paardeberg in February, 1900, because it would have given the Boers time to perfect their military defenses, and receive reënforcements, which, it was thought, were marching to relieve them; and in the same year, a similar request was refused by the British commander, Sir Archibald Hunter, because the delay might have enabled the Boers to escape from the British columns that were upon the point of surrounding them.[223]

The plea of military necessity has been employed to excuse the seizure, requisition, destruction, and devastation of enemy property. The Hague Rules of 1907 declare that private property is to be respected,[224] and that the destruction and seizure of the enemy's property is forbidden, unless it be "imperatively demanded by the necessities of war."[225] Thus by Article XXIII of the Second Hague Convention it is tacitly recognized that pressing military necessity will excuse the seizure and destruction of public and private property of the enemy as a necessary incident to the accomplishment of definite offensive or defensive military operations, or the action of a military commander of an army of occupation in making use of enemy property as a necessary incident to the effective administration of the country.[226] It may also include the destruction of any kind of property unless military necessity itself shall require its exemption, and the only exemption that military necessity has deemed it essential to make, has been in favor of those sanitary and medical units which have been specifically exempted by the provisions of the Geneva and Red Cross Conventions. It is true that such destruction must have as its object the weakening of the military forces of the enemy,[227] but this is a broad statement, and since each belligerent is, in the first instance at least, largely its own judge of its own military needs, it follows that the argument of military necessity has been employed to excuse the seizure of all kinds of military supplies in public or private hands on the ground that such action has been necessary in order to weaken the armed resistance of the enemy: — it will excuse the removal or destruction of all property situated within the hostile zone if such action is essential in order successfully to carry out the purposes of attack or defense, — even to the extent of the destruction of public buildings and religious institutions and hospitals, although in the last case Spaight points out that the commander should "provide for the patients elsewhere." [228] Military necessity might go even farther and excuse the destruction of crops and forests of standing timber, and if the necessity be sufficiently great, the destruction of towns and the devastation of whole districts. "It would even be impossible," declares Hall, "to deny to an invader the right to cut the dykes of Holland to save himself from such a fate; but when, as in the case supposed, the devastation is extensive in scale and lasting in effect, modern opinion would demand that the necessity should be extreme and patent." [229] Thus the case for the destruction of lines of communication and food supplies under plea of necessity, is much clearer than in the case of forests of standing timber, or such permanent works of engineering as dykes or levees. Only the most extreme and dire urgency, as that of a belligerent fighting for its very existence, would warrant such general devastation.

Military necessity will, as we have intimated, excuse the destruction of all means of transportation and communication within enemy territory on the ground that they are vital instruments of warfare. It therefore follows that when an army of occupation has established itself in complete and undisputed possession of a territory, the civil population has no right to interfere with lines of communication or transportation that have passed completely into the hands of the enemy; and military necessity will excuse the action of the army of occupation in holding the inhabitants within the occupied area responsible for such damage as they may commit against these lines and the commission of acts of retaliation against them for such damages. But military necessity will not excuse the execution of such punishment if the territory is not fully conquered and if it is still subject to raids from enemy forces, or if it can be fully established that a particular group of inhabitants have not committed the interference of which they have been accused.[230] It is essential that such harsh treatment of the civil population be held within the strictest limits.

Military necessity will not only excuse the destruction within the war zone of war materials, public and private property, and means of transportation and communication; but it will also excuse the destruction of all buildings, shops and factories which may be used to supply the enemy with the means of carrying on the war, and also private houses which may be used to shelter the enemy's troops. Military necessity may, therefore, excuse the destruction of entire towns and cities. Thus, for example, it was used to excuse the burning of Atlanta by General Sherman in the American Civil War: — he could not spare troops to hold the town and he could not afford to leave it standing in his rear to be seized by the enemy, and so the inhabitants were driven out of the city and it was burned to the ground.[231] It may also excuse the destruction of whole districts, such, for example, as General Sheridan's destruction of property in the Shenandoah Valley in the American Civil War,[232] the British destruction of the Boer provinces in the South African War,[233] and the complete devastation carried out by the Germans in their evacuation of the Somme front in March, 1917, and their general retreat in the autumn of 1918.

The normal rule of international law in its relation to requisitions and contributions was doubtless stated with more or less precision in Article LII of the Hague Regulations of 1907: —

"Requisitions in kind and services shall not be demanded from municipalities or inhabitants except for the needs of the army of occupation. They shall be in proportion to the resources of the country, and of such a nature as not to involve the inhabitants in the obligation of taking part in military operations against their own country.

"Such requisitions and services shall only be demanded on the authority of the commander in the locality occupied.

"Contributions in kind shall as far as possible be paid for; if not, a receipt shall be given and the payment of the amount due shall be made as soon as possible." [234]

The rule implies that requisitions shall be demanded from municipalities or inhabitants; but circumstances of extreme necessity will doubtless excuse the seizure of requisitions of kind without demand. Thus, for example, during the American Civil War, General Sherman, in his campaign in Georgia and the Carolinas, was accustomed to secure supplies without demand by foraging, on the ground that "the country was sparsely settled, with no magistrates or civil authorities who could respond to requisitions, as is done in all wars of Europe; so that this system of foraging was indispensable to our success." [235]

During the World War Germany maintained that circumstances of military necessity had forced her to adopt a system of requisition in regard to Belgium that differed widely from its normal and even exceptional exercise in most modern wars. She shipped home large quantities of supplies and also transported large groups of Belgian workers to labor in the German mines and factories.[236] As an excuse Germany pointed to the shortage of her supplies at home, and also declared that it would be dangerous to leave these supplies in the hands of a hostile population in the rear of her army, — an argument which resembles the one made by Sherman to excuse the destruction of Atlanta. Germany also argued that her conduct should be excused as a necessary reprisal for the violations of the law of blockade committed against her by England.[237] This argument is certainly of doubtful validity, — it would be difficult to prove that Germany had a right to hold Belgium responsible for a wrong committed by England against Germany. Even in time of war and among allies, such responsibility is individual and not joint. This last argument is also weakened by Germany's violation of Belgium at the outbreak of the war.

Military necessity will also excuse the adoption of certain measures of concentration for the non-combatants of the belligerent state when it is vitally essential for the success of the military operations of the belligerent instituting such measures; and also when the exigencies of the military situation may require the adoption of such measures to protect the non-combatants from greater evils which may befall them. Thus the plea of military necessity was advanced by General Kitchener to excuse the establishment of concentration camps for the non-combatants of the Boer War. It was pointed out that the isolated families were engaged in transmitting vital military information to the combatant Boers.[238] It is to be doubted, however, if the Boer situation constituted a case of genuine military necessity.[239]

The writer now proposes to consider the extent to which the rules of law may be said to impose limitations upon the practice of alleged acts of military necessity. From an examination of the cases in which the plea has been employed, there would appear to be no question that its lawful exercise should be confined to those cases in which it can be clearly shown that the law of war has given a prior sanction to its use; and when the plea has been employed to excuse the commission of certain acts not directly associated with military operations in the first instance, such as the pacific intercourse of belligerents, the seizure, requisition, destruction, and devastation of enemy property, and the treatment of non-combatants, it ought, if possible, to be held within limits that are still more strict. In the case of the pacific intercourse of belligerents, such acts ought to be examined with the most watchful scrutiny lest they result in a general relaxation of the laws of war, accompanied with acts of retaliation and reprisal, and postpone and make more difficult the return of peace. War ought largely to be limited to a conflict between the armed forces of the belligerents, and the persons and property of non-combatants ought as far as possible to be spared from its rigors. Such, indeed, had been the general tendency in the development of the rules of warfare for more than a century prior to 1914. It is true that the practice of the World War witnessed a sad departure from this tendency, and the plea of necessity was employed to excuse the commission of acts against the persons and property of non-combatants that were wholly devoid of justification. But in this case the practice of states was neither lawful nor just.

It may also be said that the fear of reprisal may impose certain limitations upon the practice of military necessity. In fact the exercise of reprisal itself has at times been excused on the ground of military necessity. Thus a Resolution of the Institute of International Law refers to the "grave cases in which reprisals appear to be absolutely necessary."[240] We are here, however, dealing with the problem of the extent to which reprisals may impose a check upon the exercise of unlawful conduct committed under plea of an alleged military necessity. That the threat or practice of reprisal has at times had this effect would appear to be unquestioned. Thus in the Franco-Prussian War, and again in the Boer War, the plea of military necessity was advanced by the invaded states to excuse the commission of acts of war against the enemy on the part of civilian inhabitants. In both cases the invaders resorted to acts of reprisal that had a marked effect in restraining the inhabitants through fear. Thus German commanders in the Franco-Prussian War compelled prominent French citizens to travel upon trains in the occupied districts of France in order to prevent wrecks;[241] and a similar practice was employed by the British against the Boers in the war in South Africa.[242] At the same time it should be pointed out that the number of cases in which such a situation can be clearly established are relatively few. It must first be established that the action of one belligerent constituted a genuine case of military necessity; and that its conduct was actually modified by the threat or practice of reprisals on the part of the other. Such cases are not only difficult to establish, but it must also be admitted that they constitute a most unsatisfactory limitation upon the practice of necessity: — there is always the danger that the act of reprisal will be more severe than is warranted by the circumstances; and it generally punishes the innocent instead of the guilty.[243]

The question may also be raised as to whether a state may not be impelled to keep its exercise of acts committed under plea of military necessity within lawful limits by the fear of an award of damages against it by an international tribunal at the close of the war. Here, again, the evidence is chiefly negative. But it is certainly not the purpose of the writer to imply that the recognition of the legal limitations which appear to constitute a part of the law of military necessity will exert any appreciable influence upon the tendency of states to violate them. The writer agrees with Hall that we should not indulge in the delusion "that formulas are stronger than passions."[244] The most that can be said is that the possibility of an award of damages by an international tribunal against a state that has violated these limitations may act in some slight degree as a check against their flagrant disregard. As between belligerents, however, such charges will not, as a rule, be lodged against the victors; and the vanquished will make every effort to evade payments.

VII

NECESSITY AND NAVAL WARFARE

THE problem of military necessity in naval warfare may be considered in a manner similar to the one employed in the preceding chapter — that is, it may be considered in connection with naval operations themselves, and secondly, in connection with matters that are not so directly concerned with naval operations. In the first group of cases the plea of military necessity has been raised chiefly in connection with coast warfare, belligerent forces, belligerent measures, belligerent instrumentalities, belligerent attack, prisoners of war, and sick, wounded and shipwrecked persons. In the second group of cases the plea of military necessity has been raised chiefly in connection with exemptions from belligerent capture and the visit and search and capture and destruction of neutral merchantmen.

The plea of necessity in its relation to coast warfare has been employed to excuse certain exceptional conduct in the treatment of lawless communities, or so-called uncivilized states, that have been unable or unwilling to perform their international obligations. The writer has already pointed out that the plea of necessity was advanced to excuse the action of the United States in the destruction of the lawless and irresponsible community at Greytown but gave as his opinion that the action taken in that case was ruthless and excessive.[245] As another example of the use of the plea of necessity against a community unable or unwilling to perform its international obligations, may be cited the naval demonstrations against Japan to compel it to obey the treaty obligations which it had recently contracted with certain states of the Western World. It would doubtless be more accurate to characterize this incident as a form of intervention; but it was also, in effect, an act of war. In June, 1863, the American steamer, *Pembroke,* while attempting to pass through the Straits of Shimonoseki, on her way from Yokohama to Nagasaki, was attacked by Japanese shore batteries and an armed brig belonging to the Japanese Prince of Nagato. The representatives of France, the United States, Great Britain and the Netherlands then signed a memorandum, declaring that " it is indispensable for the maintenance of the rights secured by the treaties concluded with Japan, to proceed immediately with the reopening of the inland sea, unobstructed until now; the free access to which has now been unexpectedly interrupted through the offensive aggressions of which the Prince of Nagato has been guilty. . . . With this object and also in view of the protection of their countrymen at the opened ports, the said representatives declare that it appears necessary to them to establish a combined action of the naval and military forces available in these seas." It was added, however, that the Government of Japan should first be warned and given an opportunity to make reparation.[246] The action of the American minister was approved by Mr. Seward, the American Secretary of State, and he was told that he might cooperate with the other Western Powers " when there is need, with reference to common defense, or to save a common right, or secure a common object, just and lawful in itself. . . ."[247]

Subsequently, in September, 1864, the United States, Great Britain, France and the Netherlands joined in a hostile demonstration against the Prince of Nagato, destroyed some shore batteries that he had erected to command the Straits of Shimonoseki and compelled him to surrender. A treaty was later concluded with the Japanese Government by which it was agreed to pay all claims for past aggressions and all the expenses incurred by the operations of the allied fleets.[248] An amount in excess of actual expenses incurred was later returned by the United States. The plea of necessity in this case would appear to have been justified on the ground that such action was required to assist the Japanese Government in maintaining its own treaty obligations. The Tycoon of Japan had been unable to make his vassal, the Prince of Chosen, observe the treaty, but he did not oppose the action of the intervening states. The plea of necessity, therefore, would appear lawfully to have been raised in extenuation and excuse of the action taken. The writer has already intimated that the action of the Powers was, in effect, an intervention, and the plea of necessity in this case is, therefore, to be judged by those considerations which the writer has discussed in connection with necessity in its relation to intervention.[249]

The problem of necessity in its relation to belligerent forces engaged in maritime warfare is conditioned by certain important factors. Unlike land warfare, it is the ship rather than the individual that constitutes the vital unit. With a splendid outward disregard of consistency, but with a purpose that is intelligible enough when it is explained on the basis of the necessities of national defense, we see a tendency for certain states that held such definite views on the problem of regular troops versus a volunteer army, to reverse themselves on the question of naval defense. Germany and Russia, though having compulsory service and large standing armies, were leaders in movements to initiate volunteer navies: — they were states with small navies, without naval traditions or proper maritime boundaries, and they were forced to depend upon their ability to make hasty naval provisions in time of danger.

It is true that the Hague Conference of 1907 endeavored more or less definitely to regulate the character of belligerent ships of war.[250] But the element of military necessity still remains in the problem in the sense that these provisions do not exclude vessels that do not comply with these conditions from engaging in hostilities in self-defense.[251]

The problem of military necessity in its relation to belligerent measures in naval warfare has arisen chiefly in connection with the bombardment of undefended places, war zones and areas of hostilities; and in its relation to belligerent instrumentalities, it has arisen chiefly in connection with the use of automatic contact mines and submarines. The Hague Conference of 1907 declared that: — "The bombardment by naval forces of undefended ports, towns, villages, dwellings, or buildings is forbidden." [252] It is, however, declared in Article II that military works, military or naval establishments, depots of arms or war *matériel*, workshops or plants which could be utilized for the needs of the hostile fleet or army, and the ships of war in the harbor, are not included in this prohibition; [253] and military necessity may be held responsible for the fact that the commander is excused from responsibility " for any unavoidable damage which may be caused by a bombardment under such circumstances." [254] Military necessity would also appear to be responsible for the declaration that undefended towns may be bombarded if they " decline to comply with requisitions for provisions or supplies necessary for the immediate use of the naval force before the place in question." [255] In carrying out a bombardment the belligerent is bound to " spare as far as possible " buildings devoted to public worship, art, science, and charity.[256] This would tend to indicate, however, that circumstances of military necessity similar to those which we have described in connection with land warfare [257] would excuse their incidental destruction. It is also declared that: — "If the military situation permits, the commander of the attacking naval force, before commencing the bombardment, must do his utmost to warn the authorities."[258] There is thus a clear implication to the effect that circumstances of military necessity will excuse the action of the commander in failing to warn the authorities.

During the World War Great Britain seems to have declared, in effect, that circumstances of military necessity required that she resort to the exceptional measure of mining the North Sea.[259] She also argued that such action constituted an act of reprisal against the alleged sowing of mines by Germany along certain trade routes of the high seas.[260] Germany, also, advanced the plea of military necessity to excuse the establishment of her war zone decrees of 1915 and 1917.[261] It is impossible, however, to see how Great Britain's plea of exceptional necessity can be accepted as a legal excuse; and it is even more impossible to accept such a plea as a legal excuse in the case of the German decrees. The latter involved such serious destruction of neutral life and property through the sinking of neutral merchant vessels by submarines, without making adequate provision for the safety of the passengers and crew, that it is impossible to devise a legal excuse for such conduct. Such acts were in plain violation of the laws of warfare as they existed prior to 1914, and in no case had the plea of necessity been permitted to give an express sanction for their use. Even to the extent that these acts are viewed as reprisals they were also clearly illegal; it is a sound rule of international law governing all reprisals the effect of which is not confined to the enemy, that they must not inflict an unreasonable degree of hardship and inconvenience upon neutral states and their subjects.[262]

The problem of necessity in its relation to instruments of naval warfare may be considered in connection with its relation to automatic contact mines and submarines. The problem is, however, essentially one of conflict between the alleged necessities of belligerents, which have not yet been definitely recognized by the rules of international law, and the lawful rights of neutrals. At the Hague Conference of 1907, it was pointed out that it was essential that neutrals should be protected against the dangers of automatic contact mines. The Chinese delegates, for example, pointed to the fact that in the recently concluded Russo-Japanese War a large number of fishing boats and coasting vessels belonging to neutrals had been destroyed by these mines, and five or six hundred neutrals engaged in peaceful pursuits had in this way lost their lives.[263]

The Conference then went upon record to the effect that " the existing position of affairs " made it impossible to forbid the employment of such mines; but it also declared that their use should be restricted and regulated in order to mitigate the severity of war and as far as possible, to protect peaceful navigation.[264] It was agreed that there should be an absolute provision against the use of such anchored mines as do not " become harmless as soon as they have broken loose from their moorings." [265] It was also forbidden to lay anchored mines off the coast or ports of the enemy " with the sole object of intercepting commercial shipping." [266] It was also stipulated that when anchored mines are used " every possible precaution must be taken for the security of peaceful shipping "; [267] and that: — " The belligerents undertake to do their utmost to render these mines harmless within a limited time and should they cease to be under surveillance, to notify the danger zones as soon as military exigencies permit." [268] It was also stipulated that unanchored mines must not be laid " except when they are so constructed as to become harmless one hour after the person who laid them ceases to control them." [269] In order, however, more adequately to defend the rights of belligerents, there was introduced a saving clause to the effect that Powers not yet possessing perfected mines of the description contemplated by the Convention were exempted from the provisions and were merely required to convert the *matériel* of their mines as soon as possible in order to bring it into conformity with the above-mentioned requirements.[270]

The events of the World War proved conclusively that these provisions failed adequately to provide for the defense of neutral rights. In the first place it should be observed that the most powerful naval state, Great Britain, ratified the Convention with a stipulation to the effect that the fact of its failure to deny the validity of certain clauses must not be considered a denial of its later right to do so. So far as England was concerned, therefore, the law remained practically in its customary state. The Convention contained no provision against the laying of mines on the high seas, and on the ground of the necessities of belligerent defense, it gave the belligerent the right to lay anchored contact mines in his own waters or in the waters of the enemy. The fact that it is forbidden to lay these mines in enemy waters " with the sole object of intercepting commercial navigation " may be overcome by the ability of the belligerent to allege a military necessity which it would be well-nigh impossible to disprove. The attempt to protect the rights of neutrals by the requirement that where mines cease to be under observation, the danger zones must be made known, is greatly weakened by the qualifying phrase, " as soon as military exigencies permit."

During the World War both Germany and England,— and the United States after its entrance into the war,— violated neutral rights by mining large portions of the high seas and by the establishment of barred zones which led to the loss of much neutral life and property. Each belligerent charged the other with being the first to initiate the practice and alleged that it was compelled to adopt such a system in self-defense.[271] Military necessity may have excused their action in adopting such measures against each other; but it is difficult to see how this plea can be used to excuse the gross violation of neutral rights that was entailed by it. The right of neutrals to take any action that might have been essential to defend themselves against these violations would have been unquestioned. Neutrals might have excused an occasional lapse of this kind under pleas of dire necessity, but the conduct of the belligerents was carried out with deliberation and was prolonged and systematic.

During the World War Germany declared that she was forced by necessity to resort to her method of submarine warfare — which involved a failure, in certain times, at least, to take sufficient care to ascertain the true character of the vessel, and to make sufficient provision for the safety of the passengers and crew, as required by the rules of international law — as a form of reprisal or retaliation for the unlawful acts of Great Britain in establishing mined and blockaded areas upon portions of the high seas.[272] The United States, as a neutral, denied the validity of this argument, and declared that such action on the part of Germany constituted "an unpardonable offense against the sovereignty of the neutral nation affected."[273] The fact that Germany's action was said by her to be in retaliation for the illegal acts of Great Britain, may help to explain her conduct, but does not give it a legal justification and excuse. We must again remember to distinguish between self-preservation as a matter of national policy, and those forms of self-preservation that have been recognized by international law. The weight of evidence points clearly to the fact that the German plea must be considered as a defense of a national policy and not of an international right. It is also clear that the unlawful conduct of Germany gave the United States a lawful reason, if such were needed, for entering the war in defense of its legal rights.

The problem of necessity in its relation to maritime attack concerns itself chiefly with military necessity in its relation to the destruction of unarmed merchant vessels. It may be stated as a general rule that unarmed merchant vessels are normally exempt from belligerent attack if they do not resist the rights of a belligerent in regard to visit and search; but at the same time, circumstances of military necessity will doubtless excuse the action of a belligerent in attacking and destroying them.[274] Thus it has been held that military necessity will justify their destruction (1) when it is not possible to keep the vessel afloat owing to her condition or unfavorable weather conditions; (2) when the vessel cannot keep up with the warship making the capture or having her in charge and might easily be recaptured by the enemy (3) when the approach of a superior enemy force creates fear of recapture; (4) when the captor cannot put on board an adequate crew without reducing his own beyond what is essential for his own safety; (5) when the port to which it would be possible to take the captured vessel is too distant.[275]

It is well established, however, that in case of the destruction of the ship by reason of necessity, every effort must be made to save the passengers, crew, and ship's papers — that the plea of necessity will not, in other words, excuse their destruction. In the World War this question was revived in active form in connection with the submarine policy pursued by Germany. Germany argued that in the conduct of her submarine warfare she did not dare to approach the defensively armed merchant ships for fear of being fired upon; and even if she did not encounter this danger and were able to take physical possession of the vessel, she still had no facilities on board the submarine for receiving the passengers and crew. She therefore contended that as a result of these new conditions of warfare, military necessity at times compelled her to destroy enemy merchantmen before she was able to make complete provision for the safety of the passengers, crew, and ship's papers.[276]

In defense of Germany's position it may be said that it is conceivable that certain circumstances might arise under which by virtue of *national* necessity and self-defense, a belligerent submarine would be justified in the destruction of enemy merchant ships without first having made complete provisions for the safety of the passengers, crew, and ship's papers. If the merchant ship is well armed and incapable of subjection, or if it is temporarily brought to bay but is still in a condition to present a renewed defense against recapture and thus to constitute itself a standing menace against submarine warfare in that particular zone of hostilities, it is possible that under these circumstances the belligerent submarine, as a measure of national defense, would be justified in ordering the passengers and crew to the open boats even though provisions for their complete safety had not been made in advance. If, again, at the moment of capture the belligerent submarine descried an armed cruiser of the enemy making for the scene of hostilities, it is also possible that the necessities of national defense would justify the submarine in ordering the passengers and crew to the open boats on the ground that such action was essential in order to prevent a rescue by the armed forces of the enemy. It may even be urged that under the present rules of maritime warfare, the safety of passengers who have embarked upon the ship of a belligerent state is largely a relative matter. It is evident that in accordance with the present rules of international law, there is nothing to prevent a submarine from destroying the passengers and crew who were formerly the occupants of a merchant vessel, together with their rescuers, as soon as they have been transferred to the deck of the enemy's armed cruiser.

In spite of this fact, however, the weight of authority would appear to hold that, according to the rules of international law as they existed prior to and during the period of the World War, it would require a case of rare and extreme necessity to furnish justification in international law for the destruction of an unarmed merchantman, without making provision — of a temporary nature, at least, — for the safety of the passengers and crew. Nor would it seem that the theory and practice of the Central Powers had as yet effected any appreciable change in favor of the doctrine which they defended. At least one international convention held since the World War, the Washington Arms Conference, went on record as strongly opposed to any modification of the present rule, and still maintained that: — " A merchant vessel must not be destroyed unless the crew and passengers have first been placed in safety." [277] It would, nevertheless, appear that the entire problem calls for reconsideration and a more detailed examination that can be given within the limits of this treatise.

The problem of military necessity in its relation to prisoners of war in maritime warfare does not differ essentially from the situation which we have described in connection with land warfare. The problem of military necessity in its relation to sick, wounded and shipwrecked persons, is, however, a matter that deserves a brief examination. The Hague Conference of 1907 aimed to impose certain restrictions upon the conduct of hospital ships, and declared that such ships belonging to neutral countries " shall afford relief and assistance to the wounded, sick and shipwrecked of the belligerents without distinction of nationality." [278] But that the use of these ships is to be strictly subordinate to the exigencies of military necessity may be seen from the provisions declaring that: — " These vessels must in no wise hamper the movements of the combatants; " [279] and: — " During and after an engagement they will act at their own risk and peril." [280] Further proof that the exigencies of military necessity are not to be subordinated to the conduct of hospital ships may be seen in the provision that: — " The belligerents shall have the right to control and search them; they can refuse to keep them, order them off, make them take a certain course, and put a commissioner on board; they can even detain them if important circumstances require it." [281]

Article VII of the Convention declares that: — " In the case of a fight on board a warship, the sick wards shall be respected as far as possible." [282] This article contains, therefore, a clear implication to the effect that circumstances of military necessity may justify the imposition of certain limitations upon the normal right of protection. The same article, after declaring that the sick wards and the *matériel* belonging to them, " cannot . . . be used for any purpose other than that for which they were originally intended, so long as they are required for the sick and wounded," [283] then adds: — " The commander, however, into whose power they have fallen may apply them to other purposes, if the military situation requires it, after seeing that the sick and wounded on board are properly provided for." This, it is plain, is another recognition of a limitation imposed by military necessity. That it is, in fact, a recognition of military necessity is also pointed out by the editor of the text of the Hague Rules used by the writer.[284] Article XVI declares that: — " After every engagement, the two belligerents, so far as military interests permit, shall take steps to look for the shipwrecked, sick, and wounded, and to protect them, as well as the dead, against pillage and ill-treatment."[285] This contains an implication to the effect that circumstances of military necessity similar to those discussed in connection with the relief of the sick and wounded in land warfare will justify a failure to make immediate provision for them.

The writer has already pointed out that in the second general group of cases, the plea of military necessity has been employed chiefly in connection with exemptions from belligerent capture and visit and search, and the capture and destruction of neutral merchant vessels. The first of these situations will now be briefly considered; the others, involving, as they do, a discussion of necessity in its relation to neutral rights, will be analyzed in connection with necessity in its relation to neutrality.

The problem of necessity in its relation to exemptions from capture has been raised chiefly in connection with fishing vessels, and small boats engaged in local trade. As a matter of normal law, these vessels are exempt from capture, but it may be argued as a principle of international law that circumstances of military necessity will sometimes excuse their capture. Thus the plea of military necessity was employed by Napoleon to excuse his seizure of Channel fishing boats in connection with his projected invasion of England;[286] and by England during the Crimean War to excuse her destruction of fishing boats and large quantities of fishing supplies in the Sea of Azov.[287] The rule of military necessity in this connection appears to have been correctly stated by the court in the case of *The Paquete Habana,* when it declared that: — "The exemption, of course, does not apply to coast fishermen or their vessels, if employed for warlike purpose, or in such a way as to give aid or information to the enemy; nor when military or naval operations create a necessity to which all private interests must give way."[288]

We may say, finally, that the limitations that may be imposed upon the practice of necessity in naval warfare, both in law and in the circumstances of external fact, would appear to be similar to those that have been discussed in considerable detail in the preceding chapter.

VIII

NECESSITY AND NEUTRALITY

One of the most important phases in the development of the law of neutrality has been the desire of belligerents to prevent third parties from extending aid to the enemy; and at the same time, and in the face of this opposition, the desire of neutrals to continue their trade that has been interrupted by the war. A logical outcome of this conflict of interest, for such it may be termed, has been an attempt to harmonize the conflicting aims of the two parties into a more or less definite body of substantive law, — the law of neutrality, — enjoining certain rights and duties upon neutrals and belligerents. Thus — to cite an important example — the law of neutrality has enjoined upon neutrals the duty of impartiality in the sense of abstaining from any conduct which shall interfere with the operation of the war as conducted by either belligerent; and at the same time it has enjoined upon belligerents the corresponding duty of respecting the position which neutrals are obliged to take, so that belligerents must not only acquiesce in the decision of neutrals to remain impartial, but they are also bound to respect that attitude in the sense of refraining from any action that would tend to treat third states as a party to the war.

Such is the general nature of the normal law of neutrality. It is the purpose of the writer in this chapter to examine the question of whether the plea of necessity may lawfully be employed to excuse a departure from the normal rights and duties that are imposed upon neutrals and belligerents in their relations with each other.

The plea of necessity in its relation to neutrality has been raised chiefly in connection with necessity in its relation to neutral rights in belligerent territory, upon the high seas, and in relation to its own national jurisdiction, and also in its relation to neutral duties within these areas.

The plea of military necessity has rightfully been employed to excuse the exercise of certain acts against the person and property of neutrals within belligerent territory. Thus it has been pointed out that it will excuse the belligerent in imposing exceptional measures of restraint upon the right of diplomatic correspondence possessed by the representatives of neutral states; [289] and it will doubtless excuse the exercise of exceptional measures in the punishment of unneutral military service rendered within the territory of the belligerent. Punishment for the commission of unneutral acts may, indeed, be said to have the sanction of normal law provided such punishment is not unduly harsh and discriminatory; but it has been pointed out that in exceptional circumstances the plea of "self-defense will justify a good deal of severity." [290]

The plea of military necessity has also been advanced to excuse the seizure, use, and even destruction of neutral property that is only temporarily within the territory of the belligerent state. Thus the weight of authority would appear to point to the fact that a state has the right to requisition foreign ships and air-craft, and other means of transportation, which are urgently required, and which are within the territorial jurisdiction at the time of requisition. It is clear that such requisition can only be made in time of a great national emergency and that it is subject to the payment of full compensation.[291] It is also clear that the plea of military necessity could not be employed to excuse the requisition of the services of foreign crews attached to such means of transportation.[292]

The plea of necessity, as an excuse for the requisition of ships and cargoes temporarily within the jurisdiction of a Prize Court, and prior to adjudication, has also been recognized in a number of judicial decisions in modern times. One of the leading cases in this connection is that of *The Curlew, Magnet* and Others.[293] The ships in question, together with their cargoes, had been seized by the British during the early days of the War of 1812 and had been brought into Halifax for adjudication. The British military and naval authorities on the station thereupon presented a petition for leave to requisition some of the ships and a portion of the cargoes pending adjudication on the ground that such action was required by circumstances of urgent necessity. Dr. Croke of the Prize Court upheld the validity of the plea in a number of cases. He declared that: — ". . . there are certain cases of necessity, in which the right of self-defense, the first law of nature and of nations, supersedes all inferior rights, and dispenses with the usual modes of proceeding. To provide for such extraordinary cases, a directionary power must of necessity, and from the nature of things, be entrusted to those to whom the application and the execution of those laws is committed. Such cases must form exceptions to the general rule of the law of nations, by which the mere *custodium inutile* is assigned to the capturing nation before the decision of the proper tribunal. They must form a case which must be fairly understood to be comprehended under the discretionary power given to the Court of Admiralty, either by the general law, or by the provisions of the Acts of Parliament. Acting, therefore upon the basis of what he held to be this discretionary power of the Court, he declared that such a case had in fact arisen and he, accordingly, granted the prayers of the petitioners: (1) as to certain small arms "very much and immediately needed for the defense of the province"; (2) as to certain oak timbers of which there was "great want" in His Majesty's naval yard at Halifax; and (3) as to a vessel immediately required for use as a prison ship. The appraised value of the property requisitioned was ordered to be brought into court.

The question again came up for adjudication in the case of *The Zamora.*[294] In this case the plea of military necessity was advanced to excuse the requisition by the British Government of 400 tons of copper, which formed a part of the cargo of the Swedish vessel, *The Zamora,* bound from New York to Stockholm. The ship had been seized off the Shetland Islands and was in the custody of the Prize Court at the time of requisition. The case went to the Judicial Committee of the Privy Council on appeal, with the result that the decision of the lower court was reversed and the requisition was not allowed. The decision of the lower court was to the effect that it was within the power and prerogative of the Crown to make a general order for the requisition of neutral property; but it was held by the higher court that such requisitions must be made in accordance with the rules of international law and not at the dictates of municipal law. Nevertheless — and this is the point with which we are now chiefly concerned — Lord Parker in giving the decision of the Court, declared that: — "A belligerent Power has by international law the right to requisition vessels or goods in the custody of its Prize Court pending a decision of the question whether they should be condemned or released, but such right is subject to certain limitations. First, the vessel or goods in question must be urgently required for use in connection with the defense of the realm, the prosecution of the war, or other matters involving national security. Secondly, there must be a real question to be tried, so that it would be improper to order an immediate release. And, thirdly, the right must be enforced by application to the Prize Court, which must determine judicially whether, under the particular circumstances of the case, the right is exercisable." [295]

The opinion expressed in *The Zamora* — that by the rules of international law, circumstances of urgent military necessity will sometimes give the belligerent the right to make a requisition of neutral goods temporarily within his ports — was reaffirmed in the case of *The Canton.*[296] Similar action was also resorted to by the French and German military authorities during the World War and the legality of the step, subject to the payment of indemnity to neutral owners, was not questioned by their respective Prize Courts.[297] Yet the admission of its legality in these cases cannot be said to give it the character of a normal rule of law; and it should be observed that the Prize Courts clearly emphasize the fact that it is a departure from the normal rules of law and to be sanctioned solely because the existence of special circumstances of military necessity can be established.

Neither should these special requisitions of certain ships and cargoes be confused with large requisitions of shipping and the general problem of angary. Attempts made during the World War to defend the seizure of large quantities of neutral shipping upon the basis of the rules of international law, can hardly be said to have been successful; as a matter of fact such seizures for the most part were defended as the exercise of a *sovereign* and not an *international* right. Such was the plea advanced by Portugal to justify her seizure of German ships,[298] by Great Britain,[299] and by the United States in justifying her seizure of about one million tons of Dutch shipping.[300] It is believed that this plea was correctly made. The systematic seizure of such large quantities of shipping for the general purposes of prosecuting the war, and not associated with any definite military objective, would appear to be a sovereign and not an international right of self-defense; and its widespread use against neutrals in the World War would appear to point to the fact that its exercise was to be explained on the basis of the exercise of a national right of eminent domain rather than any right that has yet been the subject of regulation by the rules of international law.

The question has also been raised as to whether the plea of military necessity may not also be extended to excuse the action of a belligerent in making requisitions of neutral property which is temporarily within belligerent territory. One of the most famous cases in this connection is, of course, the Duclair incident in the Franco-Prussian War of 1870, in which the Germans seized and sank seven English colliers in the Seine in order to prevent the French gunboats from coming up the river and relieving Rouen.[301] Bismarck, in defending the German action on the ground of necessity, declared that: — " . . . the measure in question, however exceptional in its nature, did not overstep the bounds of international warlike usage . . . a pressing danger was at hand, and every other means of averting it was wanting; the case was, therefore, one of necessity which, even in time of peace, may render the employment or destruction of foreign property admissible, under reservation of indemnification." [302] It should also be observed that the English Government did not deny the validity of Bismarck's plea but confined itself to a demand that the persons whose property had been destroyed should receive compensation, and the incident was settled upon this basis.[303]

The plea of necessity as an excuse for the seizure of neutral property temporarily within belligerent territory has also been recognized by the Hague Rules in connection with railway material. Article XIX of the Fifth Hague Convention on the Rights and Duties of Neutral Powers and Persons in War on Land declares that: — " Railway material coming from the territory of neutral Powers, whether it be the property of the said Powers or of companies or private persons, and recognizable as such, shall not be requisitioned or utilized by a belligerent except where and to the extent that it is absolutely necessary. It shall be sent back as soon as possible to the country of origin.

" A neutral Power may likewise, in case of necessity, retain and utilize to an equal extent material coming from the territory of the belligerent Power.

" Compensation shall be paid by one party or the other in proportion to the material used, and to the period of usage." [304]

The problem of necessity in its relation to neutral rights upon the high seas has been raised chiefly in connection with the visit and search of neutral vessels, and the capture and destruction of neutral merchant vessels. It is, of course, self-evident that the duty of a neutral vessel to submit to visit and search does not imply that it is bound to submit without resistance to lawless acts of a belligerent that are not related to its acknowledged rights. Thus the plea of necessity will doubtless excuse the act of a neutral in seeking to defend itself against a gross violation of the right of visit and search by a belligerent. In support of this statement it may be pointed out that in the case of *The Maria,* Sir William Scott declared that: — " I don't say that cases may not occur in which a ship may be authorized by the natural rights of self-preservation to defend itself against extreme violence threatened by a cruiser grossly abusing his commission." [305] Unless, however, the act of self-defense is clearly essential for the preservation of its existence, it would seem to be wise for the neutral vessel not to endeavor to carve out the measure of its own redress, but to submit, and then present its case for damages before the courts.[306] This is especially true in recent years, when the modern merchant vessels of a neutral are seldom able to present an adequate defense against the forces at the command of a belligerent. The United States, it is true, in 1917, took steps to arm defensively its merchant ships; and this action would appear to be justified by the principle of self-defense referred to by Sir William Scott in *The Maria;* and this would also appear to be a right of self-defense recognized in international law. It was maintained, in the first place, that the unrestricted submarine warfare adopted by Germany was such a clear violation of the neutral rights of the United States as fully to justify this action on the ground of self-defense; and secondly, it was maintained that the method of attack employed by the German submarine was of such a nature as to require defensive guns and gun crews for self-preservation.[307] But proof that such action is an exceptional and not a normal exercise of the right of self-defense may be seen from the fact that the burden of proof must rest upon the resisting neutral vessel to establish that it has suffered a gross violation of the right of visit and search at the hands of the ship against whom it has acted in self-defense.

In dealing with necessity in its relation to the capture and destruction of neutral merchant vessels, it may be stated as a normal rule of international law that if it is impossible to bring in a neutral ship for adjudication, she must be released.[308] Some authorities maintain, however, that in certain extraordinary circumstances of necessity, the belligerent may resort to destruction, subject to the later payment of an indemnity. Thus it has been held that military necessity will excuse destruction when a neutral ship laden with contraband has been captured as she is about to enter a belligerent port, and is then in danger of recapture by a superior force of the enemy.[309]

The practice of states and the naval codes of certain maritime powers would appear to lend a certain amount of sanction to the plea that reasons of necessity will justify destruction. Such a plea was employed by Great Britain in her wars against Napoleon,[310] by Russia in the Russo-Japanese War,[311] and by the Central Powers in the World War.[312] Sanction for such action may also be found in the Declaration of London,[313] and in the naval codes of Russia,[314] Germany,[315] and the United States.[316] Against the recognition of the argument of necessity, it is urged that the grant of legal sanction to such a principle would tend to increase the number of unwarranted attacks against neutral shipping.[317] Some authorities also urge that since a penalty must be paid by the captors in the form of compensation — provided, of course, the ship captured was not engaged in unneutral acts — this shows that such an action is necessarily a violation of international law, and that the payment of compensation does not give the captor the right to violate the law; [318] but it may also be argued that while the duty of a captor to make compensation to an owner for an act of destruction shows that there was a certain amount of fault on the part of the belligerent, this payment may also be considered an act in extenuation and excuse for a destruction that was the subject of excuse upon the basis of a lawful necessity. We have already seen that a similar line of reasoning has been employed in connection with the requisition by belligerents of the goods of neutrals temporarily in the custody of a prize court,[319] and that the payment of an indemnity in international law does not necessarily mean that the act is not to be made the subject of a lawful excuse. A similar view appears, also, to have been adopted in the Duclair incident.[320] On the other hand, it may be pointed out that British[321] and Japanese[322] prize courts seem to oppose it, and so do the declarations of a number of international law societies, such as the Institute,[323] and the Naval War College of the United States.[324]

The question doubtless remains in an unsettled state and the student of international law will probably do best to adopt an attitude of suspended judgment. The Continental states appear to be more strongly in favor of excusing the practice upon the basis of a plea of necessity than does Anglo-American jurisprudence; but that difference is undoubtedly to be explained by the practical differences in their situations. The British have a large number of ports throughout the world where prizes may be brought for condemnation proceedings; and they have a large merchant marine which they feel must be protected against unwarranted attack; the Continental states, on the other hand, have fewer ports to which prizes may be brought and their merchant marine is not such a vital factor in their protection. That states have frequently sought to excuse destruction on the basis of expediency and for the purpose of winning a war without a scrupulous regard for its legality cannot be denied; nor has international law as yet imposed any definite limitations upon their exercise of such a practice. The weight of authority, however, appears to deny the legality of such a plea in justification and excuse as a principle of international law.

In dealing with necessity in its relation to the national jurisdiction of the neutral, nothing is more certain than the fact that, as a principle of normal law, the neutral may demand that his territory shall be free from violations by a belligerent. This principle includes the right of the neutral territory to be inviolable against use as a base of operations in any form, — direct attack, the movement of troops and supplies, and the capture and disposal of prize. The question has been raised, however, as to whether exceptional circumstances of necessity will excuse the act of a belligerent in violating this neutral right of inviolability. It has been held that such a situation may arise in case the neutral is unable or unwilling to perform its duty of protecting the belligerent temporarily within its territory from attack by another belligerent. Thus in the case of *The General Armstrong,* the arbiter, in excusing Portugal for responsibility for failure to prevent the attack upon the American vessel within her port by the British, adverted to the fact that "the weakness of the Portuguese garrison . . . and the guns . . . rendered all armed intervention on his part impossible." [325] The chief reason for the rejection of the American claim against Portugal was, it is true, the failure of the American commander to apply to the Portuguese authorities for protection; [326] but the statement above would also tend to indicate that necessity in the form of a genuine inability of the neutral to grant protection may raise a slight presumption in its favor. There may be, in other words, certain cases in which the plea of necessity will be taken into consideration for the purpose of excusing the neutral from the performance of a duty which it can be established it was in fact incapable of performing. Thus Mr. Moore points out that it is just: — to take into account a nation's resources in determining whether it has, for the purpose of discharging its obligations, either of protection or of reparation, in fact employed, in an actual sense, "all the means in its power." [327] The situation is somewhat clearer if a nation has suffered such a suspension or impairment of sovereignty as to render it incapable of performing its duty of protection. We are here concerned not with the duty of a neutral to afford protection to a belligerent within its territory, as in the case of *The General Armstrong,* but with the duty of a belligerent to protect the neutral within its territory against unjust aggression from any source. Thus when the United States pressed claims against Holland for the seizure, sequestration and confiscation of American vessels in Dutch ports in 1809 and 1810, the Dutch Government was unable successfully to plead in extenuation and excuse the fact that the seizure occurred when The Netherlands were under the actual government of France.[328] The question whether the plea of necessity will be accepted as an excuse when there is not a suspension of sovereignty, but a serious impairment of its operation, is less clear. Thus in the period immediately preceding the Peace of Amiens, a large number of claims arose on the part of citizens of the United States against Spain because of captures made by French privateers fitted out in Spain, or by French privateers in Spanish waters, or because of the condemnations made by French consuls or other French agents in Spanish jurisdiction. The Spanish Government denied its liability and rested its case, at least in part, upon the fact that it was unable to prevent the commission of these acts. The United States maintained that the inability of Spain to prevent was not established and Mr. Madison declared that in order to excuse a sovereign for permitting a violation of his neutrality it must " be shown that the force or danger which destroyed the free agency really existed and that all reasonable means were employed to prevent or remedy the evil resulting." [329] It is perhaps worthy of note that by the Treaty of February 22, 1819, the United States renounced its claims against Spain " on account of prizes made by French privateers, and condemned by French consuls, within the territory and jurisdiction of Spain.[330] Certain political considerations undoubtedly had a share in dictating the settlement; but the action of the United States amounted, in effect, to a recognition of the fact that a certain amount of validity should be attached to the Spanish plea.

As a matter of normal law a neutral state may not allow a passage to a belligerent, but on the other hand, and subject to the rules already mentioned, circumstances of belligerent necessity might overcome this neutral right. Thus, for example, if a belligerent violated the territory of a neutral, and if the neutral were unable to prevent the violation, or expel the belligerent, the other belligerent might enter the territory and take steps to prevent the violation from operating to his military disadvantage.[331]

The question has been raised as to whether the plea of necessity will excuse the action of a neutral in engaging in extra-territorial pursuit for the purpose of checking such an expedition within the territorial waters of another neutral. Lord Stowell, in the case of *The Anna,* referred to the fact that Bynkershoek appears to have defended the right of territorial pursuit and he adds: — "I confess I should have been inclined to go along with him to this extent, that if a cruiser, which had before acted in a manner entirely unexceptional, and free from all violation of territory, had summoned a vessel to submit to examination and search, and that vessel had fled to such places as were entirely uninhabited, and the cruiser had, without injury or annoyance to any party whatever, quietly taken possession of his prey, it would be stretching the point too hardly against the captor to say that on this account only it should be held an illegal capture. If nothing objectionable had appeared in the conduct of the captors before, the mere following to such a place as this is, would, I think, not invalidate a seizure otherwise just and lawful."[332] This, it will be observed, refers to a pursuit and capture in such places as were "entirely uninhabited" and such a plea could not be employed to excuse the violation of a foreign jurisdiction that was inhabited. Thus in the Terceira Affair, an expedition violated the English Enlistment Act and was pursued and seized in

Portuguese territorial waters. The British Government contended that under the circumstances it was bound by its duties as a neutral to prevent such an expedition from landing in Portugal, even if the act of prevention occurred within the dominions of Portugal. The Houses of Parliament, however, passed resolutions against the act, and the resolutions of the Commons declared that it was "neither justified by the case, nor sanctioned by the general law of nations." [333] The weight of authority also supports the position taken by the British Parliament that the plea of necessity may not be employed by a neutral to excuse an attempt to give force and effect to its neutrality laws within the territory of another state.

The situation is somewhat more complicated in the case of the right of the neutral to prohibit the capture and disposal of prizes within its territory. The general rule gives the neutral the right to demand that the act be disavowed and that restitution be made,[334] and that the ship and crew be restored,[335] and that the neutral government be paid for any losses that it may have suffered as a result of the capture.[336] In the World War, however, considerable difficulty was encountered in attempting to assess the measure of damage due a neutral government in a case where there had been a capture in neutral waters by bona fide mistake and where through circumstances of accident or necessity, the vessel had been lost or destroyed. It was the opinion of the British Prize Court that the neutral government had the right to demand the return of the survivors among the crew and the payment of expenses incident to the diplomatic appeal, but that the plea of accident or necessity should excuse the belligerent government from liability for suit in any action for damages for loss of the ship. The remedy, therefore, would appear to be in action brought by the subject of the neutral state.[337]

The problem of necessity in its relation to neutral duties is closely associated with necessity in its relation to neutral rights. The problem has arisen chiefly in connection with the national jurisdiction of the neutral. Thus the plea of military necessity has sometimes been employed by the belligerent to excuse a capture in neutral waters in cases where there has been an abuse of neutral hospitality and the neutral power by its violations of the law of neutrality has shown itself unable or unwilling to perform its neutral obligations. It has been argued that the failure of a neutral to perform its duty of prevention may in turn make it responsible for having created a situation so dangerous to the belligerent that the belligerent may employ the plea of necessity to excuse its action in entering the neutral territory in order to check the consummation of any highly dangerous movement that may be directed against itself. Thus in the case of *The Ryeshitelni,*[338] in the Russo-Japanese War, Japan endeavored to excuse her seizure of a Russian vessel in the neutral Chinese port of Chefoo, on the ground that China was unable or unwilling to perform her neutral duties, and that as a result of this situation, Japan was exposed to such serious danger as to require resort to these exceptional measures.

A similar plea was made by England during the World War in the case of *The Dresden.* It appears that in March, 1915, the German cruiser, *Dresden,* sought refuge in Cumberland Bay, within Chilean territorial waters, and asked permission to remain for eight days for the purpose of repairing her engines. Permission was denied by the Chilean Government, and she was ordered to leave within twenty-four hours or suffer internment. Five days later *The Dresden* had not left port, and at this juncture a British squadron appeared and demanded her surrender. She refused, and when the British opened fire, the captain of *The Dresden* blew up his ship. The Chilean Government thereupon protested to the British Government and Great Britain offered apology but pointed out that in view of the former abuses of Chilean neutrality by German vessels, and the inability of the Chilean Government to enforce its demands in this instance, the action of the British commander was not unwarranted.[339]

During the World War the plea of military necessity was also advanced by Germany in an attempt to justify her violation of Belgium, and by the Allies in an attempt to justify their violations of Greece and Shantung; but a brief examination of the facts is sufficient to show that the term " military necessity " is loosely employed in these cases, and that the action of the various belligerents concerned was devoid of legal justification. The German Chancellor, von Bethmann-Hollweg, in his famous speech in the Reichstag, admitted that the German invasion of Belgium was devoid of legal justification.[340] His statement is an excellent presentation of the idea of political necessity; but it is not the sense in which the doctrine of necessity is employed for the purposes of furnishing a legal justification for the departure from a normal rule of law. Had Germany been able to establish a serious violation of neutrality on the part of Belgium, then her attack upon that country would have been justified; but there is no evidence to show that Belgium had been guilty of violating any neutral duty that she owed to Germany.[341]

It is one of the ironies of the situation arising from the German violation of Belgium that a somewhat similar plea of necessity had been employed by Great Britain herself to excuse her destruction of the Danish fleet at Copenhagen in 1807. It is true that the British violation was somewhat less flagrant in its character and scope than the German violation of Belgium: — it was accompanied by a more comprehensive offer of protection and compensation; and there were no charges of a prior violation of neutrality preferred against Denmark. Nevertheless it would appear that a similar wrong had been committed in both cases, and that any attempt to make a valid distinction between them is merely an attempt to select the less flagrant of two illegal acts. There is no evidence to show that Denmark had plotted with Napoleon, or had failed in any duty that it owed to Great Britain; and in spite of the efforts of a number of British publicists to defend the action of their country, it has been condemned by the great majority of Continental writers, and would appear to be devoid of legal justification.[342]

A similar plea of necessity was also employed by the Allies during the World War to justify the invasion of Greece and Shantung. On October 2, 1915, the first of a series of contingents of British and French troops landed at Salonika. The Allies sought to justify this violation of the neutral territory of Greece by declaring that such action was taken at the suggestion of the Greek Premier, Venizelos, for the purpose of carrying out the Greco-Serbian treaty of alliance, by which Greece was bound to furnish 150,000 troops to aid Serbia in repelling any attack from Bulgaria against one or both of the contracting parties. Greece was unable to fulfill this obligation, and it was argued that the landing of these troops upon Greek soil was necessary in order to aid Serbia. Thus Sir Edward Grey, British Secretary of State for Foreign Affairs, speaking in the House of Commons, on October 14, 1915, declared that it was "through Greek territory alone that direct assistance could be given rapidly by the Allies to Serbia."[343] Subsequently Premier Venezelos declared that he had asked the Allies to land troops only in case of an actual attack by Bulgaria against Serbia, and proceeded to enter a formal protest against the occupation; but regardless of the attitude of the Greek Government, it is clear that there was no legal justification for the action of the Allies.[344] The plea of Sir Edward Grey in the House of Commons brought forth from one of the members the cry of " Another Belgium." [345]

Subsequently, on April 10, 1916, the ministries of Great Britain and France informed the Greek Government that they intended to establish naval bases upon a number of Greek islands as a " means dictated by urgent necessity." [346] In September of the same year, a number of German and Austrian vessels lying in Greek territorial waters were seized and condemned by the French Prize Court on the ground that the Greek Government, with the secret connivance of King Constantine, had permitted them to use its ports and waters for supplies and operations.[347] There can be little doubt that King Constantine was in secret sympathy with the Central Powers, and he may have committed a number of minor breaches of neutrality,[348] but, nevertheless, it may be questioned if his activities had created a situation so dangerous to the cause of the Allies as to justify the exceptional measures which they proceeded to adopt. It is still more difficult to justify the action of the Allies if we bear in mind that they, also, were guilty of violating the neutrality of Greece in the early stages of the war; they were, therefore, in no position to employ the argument of necessity in justification of their attempts to arrest the progress of a dangerous agency which they were in part responsible for having set in motion. The entire situation in Greece is not so much a case involving necessity as a series of reprisals aimed by both belligerents against each other in such a way as to involve a series of unlawful attacks against the neutrality of Greece.[349]

Neither can it be said that there was any legal justification for the Japanese violation of Shangtung. On August

24, 1914, Japan declared war on Germany. The Chinese Government, in order to impose territorial limitations upon the military operations of Japan and Germany within the German leased province of Shantung, announced, under date of September 3, 1914, the establishment of a special war zone, confining the belligerent area to a territory approximately one hundred miles west of Tsingtao.[350] But Japan did not confine her operations to this war zone established by China. On the day of this announcement, a detachment of Japanese and British troops landed at Lung Kow; on November 7, 1914, they captured Tsingtau and took possession of the Shantung railway and all lines of communication both within and beyond the war zone. Japan sought to justify her action in seizing the Shantung railway to Tsingtao by a general plea of military necessity, and also by a statement to the effect that China had been permitting Germany to employ this railway for military purposes; but there is no evidence that this was the case, and even if it were true, it would not have justified the action of Japan in extending her operations beyond the war zone to the extent of taking possession of territory and lines of communication outside its limits.[351]

It is clear, therefore, that the actions of the Allies against Greece and China were violations of neutrality for which there can be found no justification in the rules of international law; and even the action taken by Great Britain against the Chilean Government in the case of the *Dresden* would appear to be of doubtful validity.[352] Such action is to be excused on the plea of necessity — if the plea of necessity is to be employed at all in these cases to describe the situation that exists where the right of the belligerent to take action against the neutral is so clear as to be beyond dispute — in cases where there has been a flagrant violation of neutrality followed by a situation in which the action taken in violation of neutral rights is essential to preserve the life of the belligerent state. But it can hardly be said that this was the situation in the cases cited above. Cases of doubt, moreover, ought always to be decided in favor of the neutral. It ought always to be borne in mind in this connection that the plea of necessity in the sense of inability of performance has not infrequently been raised by the neutral in an effort to secure an excuse for its failure to perform its neutral duties. The writer has already pointed out that question was raised as a possible excuse for the action of Portugal in the case of *The General Armstrong* although it was not the main point upon which the decision was made.[353] A similar plea of necessity was also advanced by Chile in the World War. The French Government demanded reparations for damages from the Chilean Government for permitting Germany to bring the French steamer, *Valentine*, into the Chilean port of Juan Fernandez, and hold her there for seven days, and transfer her cargo of coal and provisions to German vessels. Chile, on the other hand, pleaded that she had exercised due diligence to prevent such a violation, and argued that she should be excused from responsibility because of the distance of the island of Juan Fernandez from the mainland, and the lack of communications. It will be recalled that the decision in the case of *The General Armstrong* was made prior to the principle laid down in the Treaty of Washington, which declared that the due diligence of a neutral must be " in exact proportion to the risks to which either of the belligerents may be exposed from a failure to fulfill the obligations of neutrality." [354] It was felt that this rule imposed excessive duties upon the neutral and this explains the substitution of the phrase " the means at its disposal " by the Hague Rules.[355] This has been interpreted to mean that the neutral is required to exercise " such diligence as can reasonably be expected if all the circumstances and conditions of the case are taken into consideration." [356] It therefore follows that there may be a certain amount of justification for the argument that a neutral may advance the plea of exceptional circumstances of necessity to excuse its failure to perform its neutral duty if it has been compelled to violate the rules of neutrality by the force imposed upon it by a more powerful belligerent. The evidence in such a case, however, ought to be clear and unmistakable and the burden of proof ought to rest upon the neutral clearly to establish that such circumstances of necessity did in fact exist in sufficient degree to warrant the granting of such an excuse.

In seeking to impose legal limits upon the exercise of the doctrine of necessity in its relation to the rights and duties of neutrality, it may be said that it is difficult to see how one can find a legal justification and excuse for a belligerent violation of neutral rights in a case where the neutral has not failed in any duty which it owed to the particular belligerent. It may be said that each owes the other a normal duty to refrain from a violation of rights that belong to the other; and that action taken as the result of the violation of such rights is not a case of necessity at all but merely the exercise of a normal and perfectly legitimate right of self-defense. If this analysis of the situation is correct, then the doctrine of necessity in its relation to neutrality may be said to be practically non-existent; and with this conclusion the writer is not inclined seriously to disagree. If, on the other hand, we are to assume its existence in a limited set of circumstances, the most that we can possibly say in favor of its validity is that the extent to which the plea is to be accepted when made by a belligerent, is to be measured by the extent to which the failure of the neutral to perform its duty is directly responsible for the exceptional need which is pleaded by the belligerent; and that the extra-legal acts for which the belligerent seeks to be excused ought not to exceed in their extent those which are barely required for his preservation in the exigencies of the situation which has been forced upon him by the neutral; and that cases of doubt ought to be resolved in such a way as to afford security to the rights of neutrals, and to place limitations upon the unlawful exercise of the plea of necessity in the type of cases under consideration. The belligerent who exceeds these limitations is engaged in the employment of methods which are not yet susceptible of measurement by the rules of international law.

IX

CONCLUSIONS

THE chief difficulty in making an analysis of the development of the doctrine of necessity has been the problem of endeavoring to determine the extent to which the plea of necessity should be given consideration for the purpose of furnishing a legal excuse for a departure from a normal rule of law. An examination of the authorities tends to indicate that the doctrine of necessity as a legal principle should be subject to the following limitations: — (a) It should be confined with all possible strictness to those circumstances in which the law has in advance given an express sanction for its use; (b) it should be confined with all possible strictness to the defense of acknowledged rights, so that, other things being equal, a decision should be rendered in favor of that side which has employed the doctrine in the defense of the more clearly acknowledged rights; (c) it should be confined to cases in which the necessity of defending the state actually exists in point of fact; and in which it can be demonstrated that the action taken is essential to the preservation and continuity of the state and its ability to continue in the full and free exercise of its rights and duties; (d) the means employed should be characterized by no greater amount of extra-legal force than is rendered obligatory by the particular circumstances of the case and the need of defending the particular rights involved; (e) the danger must be so imminent and overwhelming that time and opportunity are lacking in which to provide other and adequate means of defense; (f) other things being equal, the equities of the situation must always be considered; the principles of equity do not permit a nation, because it has gone to war, to consider the rights of other nations as having become generally subordinate to its own, or justify it either in employing the doctrine of necessity in defense of its less important rights, or in sacrificing the more important rights and the safety of an unoffending state to its exigencies; (g) the fact that a state has acted in lawful self-defense does not necessarily relieve it from financial responsibility for any excessive damage that its action has produced; and if the two states immediately concerned are unable to agree upon the measure of this damage, the matter had best be left to the equitable determination of an international tribunal.

NOTES

1. Grotius, Hugo: *De jure belli,* English translation by William Whewell, Cambridge, 1853 (cited henceforth as Whewell), Lib. II, Cap. II, VIII; Whewell: Vol. 1, pp. 242–43; Grotius, Hugo: *The Freedom of the Seas,* English translation by R. V. D. Magoffin, New York, 1916, pp. 9–10.

2. Grotius: *De jure belli,* Lib. II, Cap. II; Whewell: Vol. 1, pp. 249–50.

3. Grotius: *op. cit.,* Lib. II, Cap. II, X; Whewell: Vol. 1, p. 241.

4. Grotius: *Introduction to Dutch Jurisprudence,* English translation by Charles Herbert, London, 1845, p. 60.

5. Grotius: *De jure belli,* Lib. III, Cap. IV, IV; Whewell: Vol. 3, p. 75.

6. *Ibid.,* Lib. III, Cap. XII, I, 1; Whewell: Vol. 3, p. 229.

7. *Ibid.,* Lib. II, Cap. II, XIII, 4, 5; Whewell: Vol. 1, pp. 244–47.

8. *Ibid.,* Lib. II, Cap. II, XIII, 3; Whewell: Vol. 1, p. 244.

9. *Ibid.*

10. *Ibid.,* Lib. II, Cap. II, XIII, 4; Whewell: Vol. 1, p. 245.

11. *Ibid.,* Lib. II, Cap. II, XIII, 4; Whewell: Vol. 1, pp. 244–45.

12. *Ibid.,* Lib. II, Cap. II, VI, 2; Whewell: Vol. 1, p. 238.

13. "It may appear superfluous for us to treat of those who are extraneous to the war, since it is evident that there are no rights of war against them. But since many liberties are often taken with them, especially when they are neighbors, on the pretext of necessity, we may here briefly repeat what we have already said: — that Necessity in order to give a person a right to another's property must be of the extremest kind: — that it is further requisite, that there must not be a similar necessity on the part of the owner: — that even when the necessity is plain, more is not to be taken than it requires: that is, if keeping the thing is sufficient, it is not to be used; if using it is sufficient, it is not to be destroyed; if destroying it is requisite, the price is to be repaid." *Ibid.,* Lib. III, Cap. XVII, I; Whewell: Vol. 3, p. 288.

14. "Thomas Aquinas well says, if it be rightly taken, that a man killed in self-defense, is not killed by intention: not that sometimes, if no other way of safety appear, it may not be lawful to

do that of set purpose, which will cause the death of the aggressor, but that such death is not chosen as something primarily intended, as in judicial punishment it is, but it is chosen as the only thing which is then possible; since he who is attacked, even then ought to do anything by which the assailant may be scared away, or deprived of power, rather than by which he may be killed." *Ibid.*, Lib. II, Cap. I, IV, 2; Whewell: Vol. 1, pp. 207–8.

15. ". . . but if I am myself in danger of life, then I may repel the danger even with danger to the life of another; nor does this cease to hold, however I have come into that danger, whether by trying to retain my property, or to recover it, or to capture the thief: for in all these cases I am acting lawfully according to my right." *Ibid.*, Lib. II, Cap. I, XII, 1; Whewell: Vol. 1, p. 218. ". . . but if there be testimony by which it appears that the slayer was not in danger of his life, the presumption ceases, and he is guilty of homicide." *Ibid.*, Lib. II, Cap. I, XII, 3; Whewell: Vol. 1, pp. 219–20. ". . . or if anyone were under the necessity of defending his own person, his wife, children or property, against force or violence, and consequently killed another, which is called self-defense, in such a case he (who has without any fault of his own occasioned the death) may obtain his burgher right from the Sovereign, even without reconciliation and compensation." Grotius: *Introduction to Dutch Jurisprudence*, pp. 439–40.

16. "Present danger is here required and imminent in point of time." Grotius: *De jure belli*, Lib. II, Cap. I, V, 1; Whewell: Vol. 1, pp. 208–9.

17. ". . . even when the necessity is plain, more is not to be taken than it requires; that is, if keeping the thing is sufficient, it is not to be used; if using it is sufficient, it is not to be destroyed; if destroying it is requisite, the price is to be repaid." *Ibid.*, Lib. III, Cap. XVII, I; Whewell: Vol. 3, p. 288.

18. ". . . it is further requisite, that there be not a similar necessity on the part of the owner. . . ." *Ibid.*, Lib. III, Cap. XVII, I; Whewell: Vol. 3, p. 288. ". . . such liberty is not granted if the possessor be in like necessity. . . ." *Ibid.*, Lib. II, Cap. II, VIII; Whewell: Vol. 1, p. 240.

19. ". . . when it is possible, restitution should be made. There are some who think otherwise on this point, and consider that, as the man used his own Right, he is not bound to restitution. But it is more true that this Right was not plenary, but limited by the burthen of restoring what was taken, when the necessity was over: for such a Right suffices to preserve the natural equity of the case

against the rigor of ownership." *Ibid.*, Lib. II, Cap. II, IX; Whewell: Vol. 1, p. 240.

20. *Ibid.*, Lib. I, " Prolegomena," p. 59.

21. Macdonnell, Sir John, and Manson, Edward: *Great Jurists of the World*, Boston, 1914, p. 51.

22. Machiavelli, Niccolò: " Works," translated by Ellis Farneworth, 2d ed., London, 1775, *Letters as Secretary of State of Florence*, " Machiavelli to Fra Filippo de Louni, Chief Magistrate and Commissary of Firiziani, March 7, 1511," Vol. 4, pp. 324–25.

23. *Idem:* " Works," *op. cit.*, Vol. 4, pp. 296–97.

24. Machiavelli: *Discourses on the First Decade of Titus Livius*, translated by Ninian Hill Thompson, London, 1883, p. 473.

25. Machiavelli: " Works," *The Art of War*, Vol. 4, pp. 91–92.

26. *Ibid.*, pp. 203–4.

27. *Ibid.*

28. Morley, John: *Critical Miscellanies*, " Machiavelli," New York, 1908, Vol. 4, p. 53.

29. Hobbes, Thomas: *The Elements of Law, Natural and Political*, edited by Ferdinand Tönnies, London, 1878, p. 190; Hobbes: " Works," *De corpore politico*, ed. by Sir William Molesworth, London, 1839–45, Vol. 4, p. 228. The text of Tönnies is cited first whenever possible, because of its superiority to the text of Molesworth.

30. Hobbes: *The Leviathan*, ed. by Molesworth, Vol. 3, pp. 342–43.

31. " We see all countries, though they be at peace with their neighbors, yet guarding their frontiers with armed men, their towns with wall and ports, and keeping constant watches. To what purpose is all this if there be no fear of the neighboring power? " Hobbes: *Philosophical Rudiments*, " The Epistle Dedicatory," ed. by Molesworth, Vol. 2, p. 15.

32. Hobbes: *The Leviathan*, ed. by Molesworth, Vol. 3, p. 235.

33. *Ibid.*

34. Hobbes: *The Elements of Law*, ed. by Tönnies, pp. 100–1; Hobbes: *De corpore politico*, ed. by Molesworth, Vol. 4, p. 118; Hobbes: *The Leviathan*, ed. by Molesworth, Vol. 3, p. 305; Hobbes: *Philosophical Rudiments*, " The Epistle Dedicatory," ed. by Molesworth, Vol. 2, p. 2.

35. Hobbes: *The Leviathan*, ed. by Molesworth, Vol. 3, pp. 703–4.

36. Pufendorf, Samuel: *De jure naturae et gentium*, Frankfort and Leipsic, 1759, Lib. II, Cap. VI, p. 282 (cited henceforth as

Pufendorf). English translation by Basil Kennett, Oxford, 1710, Book II, Chap. VI, p. 160 (cited henceforth as Kennett).

37. Pufendorf: Book II, Chap. III, Sec. 11, p. 195; Kennett: Book II, Chap. III, Sec. 11, pp. 106–7.

38. Pufendorf: Book II, Chap.V, Secs. 6–8, pp. 262–66; Kennett: Book II, Chap. V, Secs. 6–8, pp. 149–50.

39. " But under civil government we are to fly if we can with convenience, rather than take away the assailant's life. . . . We added this restriction, *if we can with convenience,* because . . . we are not always obliged to retreat and to turn our backs, since we thus expose ourselves to a greater danger of wounds and mischief, as well as to the additional one of falling; and since a man who hath once betaken himself to his heels, if he meet with a stop, or if the aggressor happen to overtake him, cannot easily recover himself into a position of defense. Therefore in case there be not a place of safe refuge near at hand, he doth not transgress the bounds of innocent self-defense, who opposes an assailant breast to breast, rather than he will lay himself open to his violence by running off on a disadvantage." Pufendorf: Book II, Chap. V, Sec. 13, pp. 270–71; Kennett: Book II, Chap. V, Sec. 13, p. 154. See also Pufendorf: Book II, Chap. V, Sec. 3, pp. 257–60; Book VIII, Chap. VI. Sec. 8, pp. 438–39; Kennett: Book II, Chap. V, Sec. 2, pp. 145–46; Book VIII, Chap. VI, Sec. 8, p. 689.

40. Pufendorf: Book II, Chap. V, Sec. 4, pp. 260–61; Kennett: Book II, Chap. V, Sec. 4, pp. 147–48.

41. Pufendorf: Book VIII, Chap. VI, Sec. 8, p. 439; Kennett: Book VIII, Chap. VI, Sec. 8, p. 689.

42. Pufendorf: Book I, Chap. V Sec. 9, pp. 74–75; Book II, Chap. V, Secs. 10–11, pp. 267–68; Sec. 18, pp. 279–80; Kennett: Book I, Chap. V, Sec. 9, pp. 39–40; Book II, Chap. V, Secs. 10–11, pp. 151–52; Sec. XVIII, pp. 159–60.

43. Pufendorf: Book II, Chap. VI, Secs. 5–6, pp. 287–91; Kennett: Book II, Chap. VI, Secs. 5–6, pp. 164–66.

44. Pufendorf: Book II, Chap. VI, Sec. 8, p. 293; Kennett: Book II, Chap. VI, Sec. 8, pp. 167–68.

45. Pufendorf: Book II, Chap. VI, Secs. 5–6, p. 291; Kennett: Book II, Chap. VI, Secs. 5–6, pp. 164–66.

46. Pufendorf: Book IV, Chap. V, Secs. 7–8, pp. 541–45; Sec. 10, p. 547; Kennett: Book IV, Chap. V, Secs. 7–8, pp. 306–8; Sec. 10, p. 309.

47. Pufendorf: *De statu imperii,* 3 Zeumer, " Quellen und Studien zur Verfassungsgeschichte des d.R.," 1910, cited in Goebel,

Julius: "The Equality of States," *Columbia Law Review*, Vol. 23, pp. 274–76.

48. Hassall, Arthur: "The Foreign Policy of Louis XIV (1661–97)." *The Cambridge Modern History*, New York, 1912, Vol. 5, pp. 38–42.

49. Pufendorf: Book III, Chap. III, Sec. 5, p. 335; Kennett: Book III, Chap. III, Sec. 5, p. 192.

50. Pufendorf: Book III, Chap. III, Sec. 5, pp. 336–37; Kennett: Book III, Chap. III, Sec. 5, p. 192.

51. Pufendorf: Book III, Chap. III, Sec. 5, p. 336; Kennett: Book III, Chap. III, Sec. 5, p. 193. He declares, on the other hand, that "if we are either too weak to hinder his progress, or must on this score engage in dangerous war, the plea of necessity will fairly justify us to our neighbors." *Ibid.*

52. Pufendorf: Book III, Chap. III, Sec. 6, p. 338; Kennett: Book III, Chap. III, Sec. 6, pp. 193–94.

53. Pufendorf: Book III, Chap. III, Sec. 5, p. 336; Kennett: Book III, Chap. III, Sec. 5, p. 193.

54. Ward, Robert: *An Inquiry into the Foundation and History of the Law of Nations in Europe*, Dublin, 1795, Vol. I, pp. 176–78.

55. Pufendorf: Vol. 2, Book VIII, Chap. VI, Sec. 13, p. 444; Kennett: Book VIII, Chap. VI, Sec. 13, p. 698.

56. Pufendorf: Vol. 2, Book VIII, Chap. VII, Sec. 11, p. 456; Kennett: Book VIII, Chap. VII, Sec. 11, p. 698.

57. *Ibid.*

58. Pufendorf: Vol. 2, Book VIII, Chap. VI, Sec. 7, pp. 437–38; Kennett: Book VIII, Chap. VI, Sec. 7, p. 688.

59. Pufendorf: Book II, Chap. VI, Sec. 8, pp. 293–94; Kennett: Book II, Chap. VI, Sec. 8, p. 168.

60. Pufendorf: Vol. 2, Book VIII, Chap. II, Sec. 2, pp. 303–4; Kennett: Book VI, Chap. II, Sec. 12, p. 611.

61. Pufendorf: Vol. 2, Book VIII, Chap. II, Sec. 6, p. 309; Kennett: Book VIII, Chap. II, Sec. 6, pp. 614–15.

62. Pufendorf: Vol. 2, Book VIII, Chap. VI, Sec. 18, pp. 447–49; Kennett: Book VIII, Chap. VI, Sec. 18, p. 694.

63. Pufendorf: Vol. 2, Book VIII, Chap. VI, Sec. 6, pp. 437–38; Kennett: Book VIII, Chap. VI, Sec. 6, pp. 687–88.

64. *Supra*, pp. 12–19. One difficulty is that Pufendorf draws his illustrations chiefly from internal law.

65. Rousseau, Jean Jacques: "Political Writings," ed. by C. E. Vaughan, Cambridge, 1915, *The Social Contract*, Vol. 2, p. 30.

66. Wolff, Christian: *Jus gentium methodo scientifico pertrac-*

tatum, Magdeburg, 1749, Secs. 9–10, pp. 7–9; Sec. 156, pp. 123–24; Sec. 157, pp. 124–25; Sec. 158, p. 125; Sec. 206, pp. 162–63.

67. Vattel, Emmerich de: *The Law of Nations*, translated by Charles G. Fenwick, Washington, 1916, pp. 9–10, 93–94 (cited henceforth as Vattel).

68. *Ibid.*, pp. 8, 113–16, 130.

69. Vattel: p. 255.

70. Gentilis, Albericus: *Hispanicae advocationis libri duo*, translated by Frank Frost Abbott, New York, 1921, pp. 122–24.

71. Zouche, Richard: *Juris et iudicii fecialis*, translated by J. L. Brierly, Washington, 1911, pp. 113–14.

72. Textor, Johann Wolfgang: *Synopsis juris gentium*, text of 1680, translated by J. P. Bate, Washington, 1916.

73. Bynkershoek, Cornelius van: *De dominio maris dissertatio*, translated by R. V. D. Magoffin, New York, 1923, p. 44.

74. *Idem: Treatise on the Law of Nations*, translated by Peter Stephen du Ponceau, Philadelphia, 1810, p. 2.

75. Montesquieu, Charles Louis de Secondat: *The Spirit of Laws*, translated by Thomas Nugent, London, 1878, Vol. 1, p. 144.

76. Martens, G. F. von: *A Compendium of the Law of Nations*, translated by William Cobbett, London, 1802, p. 272.

77. *Ibid.*, p. 279.

78. *Ibid.*, p. 304.

79. Fulton, F. W.: *The Sovereignty of the Seas*, Edinburgh and London, 1911, pp. 666–67, 676, 677.

80. *The Apollo*, 9 Wheat. 177.

81. *The Hague Arbitration Cases*, ed. by George Grafton Wilson, Boston and London, 1915, pp. 179–80.

82. Hall, W. E.: *A Treatise on International Law*, 7th ed., by A. P. Higgins, Oxford, 1917, p. 266; Piggott, Sir Francis T.: *Nationality*, 2 vols., London, 1907, Vol. 2, pp. 35–40.

83. Proceedings, Fur Seal Arbitration, 15 vols., Washington, Government Printing Office, 1895, Vol. 7, p. 19; Malloy, William M.: Conventions, International Acts, Protocols and Agreements between the United States of America and Other Powers, 1776–1909, Washington, 1910–23, Vol. 1, pp. 751, 766; Foster, John W.: *Diplomatic Memoirs*, 2 vols., Boston, 1909, Vol. 2, pp. 48–49.

84. Moore, John Bassett: *A Digest of International Law*, 8 vols., Washington, Government Printing Office, 1906, Vol. 2, p. 144. See also Moore, John Bassett: *A History and Digest of the International Arbitrations to Which the United States Has Been a Party*,

6 vols., Washington, Government Printing Office, 1898, Vol. 5, pp. 5021 *et seq.*, in which a similar plea made by the Portuguese government was rejected on the ground that it had executed its exceptional measures without having given sufficient warning. This shows that a necessity must exist in fact.

85. Hall: *op. cit.*, 4th ed., Oxford, 1895, p. 203.

86. 7 Cranch 116.

87. Ortolan, Théodore: *Règles internationales et diplomatie de la mer*, 2 vols., Paris, 1864, Vol. 1, p. 218; Gregory, C. N.: "Jurisdiction over Foreign Ships in Territorial Waters," *Michigan Law Review*, February, 1904, p. 333–47.

88. Sir William Scott, in *The Eleanor*, Edwards, pp. 159, 160.

89. Benedict, Erastus C.: *The American Admiralty*, 4th ed., Albany, 1910, p. 154.

90. Moore: *Dig.*, Vol. 2, p. 349.

91. *The Major Barbour*, Blatch, *Prize Cases*, p. 467; *The Sunbeam, ibid.*, pp. 316, 656; *The Diana*, 7 Wall. 354; *The Josefa Segunda, Cassicabura, et al.*, 5 Wheat. 338 (1820); Sir William Scott, in *The Eleanor*, Edwards, pp. 159, 160.

92. *The Eleanor*, Edwards, pp. 159. 160.

93. *Ibid.*

94. Moore: *Dig.*, Vol. 2, p. 401.

95. Moore: *Dig.*, Vol. 2, pp. 402, 405–8; Vol. 6, p. 371; American State Papers, Foreign Relations: Vol. 3, p. 571; Vol. 4, pp. 130, 132, 183–84, 215, 292, 450, 463–64, 478, 539, 541, 545–46; American State Papers, Military Affairs: Vol. 1, pp. 698–708; Adams, Henry: *History of the United States*, 9 vols., New York, 1891–98, Vol. 1, pp. 438–42; Vol. 5, pp. 307–15; Moore: *Int. Arb.*, Vol. 5, pp. 4519–31; Parton, James: *Life of Jackson*, New York, 1860, pp. 451–500.

96. Moore: *Dig.*, Vol. 2, p. 420.

97. Moore: *Dig.*, Vol. 2, pp. 409–12; Hall: *op. cit.*, 7th ed., pp. 84, 279–80; Kent, James: *Commentary on International Law*, edited by J. T. Abdy, 2d ed., Cambridge and London, 1878, p. 148; Westlake, John: *International Law*, 2d ed., Cambridge, 1910, Vol. 1, pp. 313–14; Oppenheim, L.: *International Law*, 2d ed., New York, 1912, Vol. 1, p. 187; Phillimore, Sir Robert: *Commentaries upon International Law*, 3d ed., London, 1879–89, Vol. 1, p. 351; Hyde, Charles Cheyney: *International Law, Chiefly as Interpreted and Applied by the United States*, 2 vols., Boston, 1922, Vol. 1, pp. 107–8.

98. H. Ex. Doc. No. 13, 45th Cong., 1st sess., 14; H. Rep. No. 701, 45th Cong., 2d sess., 241.

99. H. Ex. Doc. No. 13, 45th Cong., 1st sess., 18–22; H. Rep. No. 701, 45th Cong., 2d sess., 242–54.

100. For. Rel. 1878, 572; For. Rel. 1879, 754; For. Rel. 1880, 726; Moore: *Dig.*, Vol. 2, p. 436.

101. Moore: *Dig.*, Vol. 2, p. 437.

102. *Annuaire*, Vol. 3, pp. 276–81; Hall: *op. cit.*, 4th ed., pp. 218–20; Moore: *Dig.*, Vol. 2, pp. 200–202; Fiore, Pasquale: in *R.D.I.P.*, Vol. 11, p. 302; Wharton, Francis: *On the Conflict of Laws*, Philadelphia, 1881, 2d ed., Secs. 809–13; Westlake: *op. cit.*, Vol. 1, pp. 251, 253; Oppenheim: *op. cit.*, Vol. 1, pp. 203–5.

103. *The Marianna Flora*, 11 Wheat. 1.

104. Moore: *Dig.*, *Vol.* 2, pp. 895–905; Hall: *op. cit.*, 4th ed., pp. 278–79.

105. Moore: *Dig.*, Vol. 2, p. 892.

106. Twiss, Sir Travers: *The Law of Nations Considered as Independent Political Communities*, Oxford and London, 1861, pp. 261–64; Hall: *op. cit.*, 5th ed., pp. 275–78; Fiore, Pasquale: *International Law Codified and Its Legal Sanction*, English translation from the 5th Italian ed., by Edwin M. Borchard, New York, 1918, pp. 387–88; Perels, F.: *Das internationale öffentliche Seerecht*, Berlin, 1903, Sec. 17; Bonfils, Henry; *Manuel de droit international public*, 7th ed., by Fauchille, Paris, 1914, Nos. 517–19, pp. 343–46.

107. Webster, Daniel: "Works," 12th ed., 6 vols., Boston, 1860, Vol. 6, pp. 347 *et seq.*

108. Mr. Cass, Secretary of State, to Mr. Dallas, Minister to England, February 23, 1859, Moore: *Dig.*, Vol. 2, p. 942.

109. Dip. Cor. 1862, 65, 141, 158, 164, 181, 185, 289, 509, 513, 573. In a note of April 10, 1858, Mr. Cass, the American Secretary of State, in speaking of the same matter, had written: "It is one thing to do a deed avowedly illegal and excuse it by the attending circumstances; and it is another and quite different thing to claim a right of action, and the right also of determining when, and how, and to what extent, it shall be exercised." Mr. Cass, Secretary of State, to Lord Napier, British Commissioner, April 10, 1858, S. Ex. Doc. No. 49, 35th Cong., 1st sess., 42, 47, 48. This seems to be an excellent definition of lawful necessity.

110. *The Marianna Flora*, 11 Wheat. 1; *The Palmyra*, 12 Wheat. 1.

111. *The Mary Lowell:* Moore: *Int. Arb.*, Vol. 3, pp. 2772–77; S. Ex. Doc. No. 108, 41st Cong., 2d sess.

112. *The Salvador*. L. R. 3 P. C. 318.

113. Hall: *op. cit.*, 5th ed., p. 276; Westlake: *op. cit.*, 1st ed., Cambridge, 1904, Vol. 1, pp. 167–69.

114. Borchard, Edwin M.: *Diplomatic Protection of Citizens Abroad*, New York, 1916, p. 52.

115. Mr. Gresham, Secretary of State, to Mr. Smythe, Minister to Hayti, Nov. 5, 1894, For. Rel., Vol. 2, p. 801; Moore: *Dig.*, Vol. 4, p. 84.

116. Borchard: *op. cit.*, p. 60.

117. Nys, Ernest: *Le droit international*, 3 vols., Brussels, 1912, Vol. 3, p. 34; Catellani: *Condizioni e effetti grundica dello stato di guerra*, Venice, 1906, p. 61.

118. 12 *Annuaire* (1892), pp. 223–24, Art. 28; see also 11 *Annuaire* (1891), pp. 310–11.

119. Bonfils-Fauchille: *op. cit.*, No. 1055.

120. Spaight, J. M.: *War Rights on Land*, London, 1911, pp. 29–31.

121. Hershey, Amos S.: *International Law in the Russo-Japanese War*, New York, 1916, pp. 269, 282.

122. Fenwick, Charles G.: *International Law*, New York, 1924, p. 446.

123. Cobbett, P. H.: *Leading Cases on International Law*, 4th ed., London, 1922, 2 vols., Vol. 1, pp. 316–18; Calvo, M. Charles: *Le droit international*, 6 vols., Paris, 1896, Vol. 6, pp. 268–70; Oppenheim: *op. cit.*, Vol. 1, pp. 466–67; Taylor, Hannis: *A Treatise on International Public Law*, Chicago, 1901, pp. 336–37; Hall: *op. cit.*, 5th ed. pp. 184–86; Martens, G. F. von: *Précis du droit des gens moderne de l'Europe*, 2 vols., Paris, 1858, Vol. 2, pp. 109–16; Martens, Karl von: *Causes célèbres du droit des gens*, 5 vols., Leipzig, 1858–61, Vol. 4, pp. 20–44; Klüber, J. L.: *Droit des gens moderne de l'Europe*, 2d ed., by M. A. Ott, Paris, 1874, Secs. 211–13; Wheaton, Henry: *Elements of International Law*, 8th ed., by Richard Henry Dana, Jr., London, 1866, Dana's note No. 129, pp. 226–28; Bluntschli, Jean-Gaspard: *Le Droit international codifié*, translated from the German by M. C. Lardy, 5th ed., Paris, 1895, Secs. 211–15; Moore: *Dig.*, Vol. 4, pp. 633, 648–69; Textor: *op. cit.*, p. 149; Vattel: *op. cit.*, pp. 379–92; Hershey, Amos S.: *Diplomatic Agents and Immunities*, Washington, 1919, pp. 144–45, 150, 156; Halleck, Henry Wager: *Inter-*

national Law, 2 vols., 4th ed., by Sir G. Sherston Baker, London, 1908, Vol. 1, pp. 363–64.

124. Oppenheim: *op. cit.*, Vol. 1, pp. 466–67.

125. Moore: *Dig.*, Vol. 4, p. 678.

126. Moore: *Dig.*, Vol. 4, pp. 695–701; Satow, Sir Ernest M.: *Guide to Diplomatic Practice*, 2 vols., London, 1917, Vol. 1, pp. 329–30, 334–37; Hershey: *Diplomatic Agents and Immunities*, pp. 23–24; Hall: *op. cit.*, 6th ed., p. 304.

127. Hall: *op. cit.*, 8th ed., p. 415.

128. Oppenheim: *op. cit.*, Vol. 1, 550.

129. Westlake: *op. cit.*, ed. of 1910, Vol. 1, pp. 316–17; Martens, G. F. von: *op. cit.*, Book IV, Chap. I, Sec. 120; Twiss: *op. cit.*, Vol. 1, Sec. 901, pp. 147–48; Creasey, Sir Edward: *First Platform of International Law*, London, 1876, pp. 152–53.

130. *Supra*, pp. 26–36.

131. *Supra*, p. 33.

132. Hall: *op. cit.*, 4th ed., Oxford, 1895, pp. 300–302; Phillimore: *op. cit.*, 3d ed., London, 1879, Vol. 1, p. 568; Martens, G. F. von: *op. cit.*, Vol 1, Sec. 75; Heffter, A. G.: *Le droit international de l'Europe*, 4th ed., by F. Heinrich Geffcken, Berlin and Paris, 1883, Sec. 45; Bluntschli: *op. cit.*, Sec. 479; Pradier-Fodéré, P.: *Traité de droit international public*, 8 vols., Paris, 1885–1906, Vol. 1, p. 478; Bonfils-Fauchille: *op. cit.*, 7th ed., Secs. 310–12; Moore: *Dig.*, Vol. 6, pp. 6–10; Hyde: *op. cit.*, Vol. 1, pp. 121–22, 124–26.

133. Oppenheim: *op. cit.*, Vol. 1, pp. 193 ff.; Phillipson, Coleman: *International Law and the Great War*, London, 1915, pp. 2–3; Wheaton, Henry: *History of the Modern Law of Nations*, New York, 1845, pp. 82–83.

134. "Any country whose people conduct themselves well can count upon our hearty friendliness. If a nation shows that it knows how to act with decency in its industrial and political matters; if it keeps order and pays its obligations — then it need fear no interference from the United States. Brutal wrongdoing, or impotence which results in the general loosening of the ties of civilized society, may finally require intervention by some civilized nation, and in the Western Hemisphere, the United States cannot ignore its duty." Letter of President Roosevelt in reference to Santo Domingo, May, 1904. Quoted in Moore, John Bassett: *American Diplomacy*, New York, 1918, pp. 261–62. See also *infra*, pp. 33–4. ". . . the . . . principle which underlies the Monroe

Doctrine; that is to say, . . . the right of every sovereign state to protect itself by preventing a condition of affairs in which it will be too late to protect itself." Root, Elihu: "Our Real Monroe Doctrine," *AJIL.*, Vol. 8, 1914, p. 432.

135. "The real cause of our national discontent is that the French army which is now in Mexico . . . could not but be regarded by the people of the United States as injurious and menacing to their own chosen and endeared republican institutions." Mr. Seward, Secretary of State, to the Marquis de Montholon, French Minister, Dec. 6, 1865, H. Ex. Doc. No. 73, 39th Cong., 1st sess., pt. 2, p. 347.

136. "British Columbia, by whomsoever possessed, must be governed in conformity with the interests of her people and of society upon the American continent." Statement of Mr. Seward in 1867, quoted in Hart, A. B.: *The Monroe Doctrine*, Boston, 1916, p. 155. "The people of the United States can not regard the proposed confederation of the provinces on the northern frontier of this country without extreme solicitude." Resolution of the House of Representatives, March 27, 1867, Dip. Cor. 1867, Cong. Globe, 40th Cong., 1st sess., p. 392.

137. "The highest and first duty of every independent nation is to provide for its own safety; and acting upon this principle, we should be compelled to resist the acquisition of Cuba by any powerful maritime State, with all the means which Providence has placed at our command." Mr. Buchanan, Secretary of State, June 17, 1848, quoted in Moore: *Dig.*, Vol. 6, p. 451. "Such a conflict waged for years in an island so near us and with which our people have such trade and business relations . . . is a constant menace to our peace and compels us to keep on a semi-war footing with a nation with which we are at peace." President McKinley, Special Message to Congress, April 11, 1898, For. Rel. 1898, p. 750; Moore: *Dig.*, Vol. 6, p. 220. "Cuba lies at our door, and whatever affects her for good or ill affects us also. So much have our people felt this that in the Platt Amendment we definitely took the ground that Cuba must hereafter have closer political relations with us than with any other power. Thus in a sense Cuba has become a part of our international political system." President Roosevelt, Message of Dec. 2, 1902, For. Rel. 1902, p. 20.

138. "As a mere matter of self-defense, we must exercise a close watch over the approaches to this [the Panama] canal; and this means that we must be thoroughly alive to our interests in the

Caribbean Sea." President Roosevelt, Annual Message, Dec. 5, 1905, For. Rel. 1905, p. 33.

139. A Senate Resolution in 1912 declared that the acquisition of territory in this region by foreign subjects, and in such places as might be available for military or naval purposes, " could not be seen without grave concern" by the United States. Cong. Record, Vol. 48, pp. 10045–57. The practice of the Great Powers in this respect has been similar to that of the United States. The same principle has been emphasized in the attitude of the Great Powers towards the Balkans and Morocco, and in the exercise of territorial jurisdiction in Asia and Africa. See *A.J.I.L.*, Supp. Vol. 6, p. 27; British and Foreign State Papers, Vol. 69, pp. 758, 1107; Vol. 91, p. 91; Hall: *op. cit.*, ed. by Higgins, p. 91; Wright, Quincy: "Territorial Propinquity," *A.J.I.L.*, Vol. 12, 1918, pp. 542–43.

140. "The present condition of affairs in Cuba is a constant menace to our peace, and . . . the lives and liberty of our citizens are in constant danger and their property destroyed and themselves ruined . . ." President McKinley, Special Message to Congress, April 11, 1898, quoted in Moore: *Dig.*, Vol. 6, p. 220. "Its intervention rested upon the ground that there existed in Cuba conditions so injurious to the United States, as a neighboring nation, that they could no longer be endured." Moore: *American Diplomacy*, ed. of 1918, p. 208.

141. Westlake: *op. cit.*, Vol. 2, pp. 312–13; Calvo: *op. cit.*, ed. of 1896, Sec. 297, p. 201; Halleck: *op. cit.*, Vol. 1, p. 120; Phillimore: *op. cit.*, Vol. 1, pp. 317–19; Rivier, Alphonse: *Principes du droit des gens*, Paris, 1897, Vol. 1, p. 277; Wheaton: *Elements of International Law*, Dana's ed., pp. 90–92.

142. *Supra*, p. 33.

143. Borchard: *Diplomatic Protection*, pp. 448–51; Moore: *Dig.*, Vol. 6, pp. 253, 259–62, 677, 683–87; Vol. 7, pp. 108, 112–17, 346–48, 354; Westlake: *op. cit.*, ed. of 1910, Vol. 1, pp. 352–55; Malloy: *Treaties*, Vol. 2, p. 2248.

144. *Infra*, pp. 51–53, 56–57.

145. President Pierce, Annual Message, Dec. 4, 1854, Richardson's Messages, Vol. 5, p. 282.

146. Moore: *Dig.*, Vol. 2, p. 414.

147. Mr. Marcy, Secretary of State, to Count Sartiges, French Minister, Feb. 26, 1857, quoted in Moore: *Dig.*, Vol. 6, pp. 935–36.

148. *Ibid.*

149. Hansard: Parl. Debates, 3d ser., CXLVI, p. 41, quoted in Moore: *Dig.*, Vol. 6, p. 939.

150. "The occurrence at Greytown is an embarrassing affair. The place merited chastisement, but the severity of the one inflicted exceeded our expectations. The Government will, however, I think, stand by Capt. Hollins." Buchanan, James: "Works," Vol. 9, p. 248, quoted in Williams, Mary Wilhelmine: *Anglo-American Isthmian Diplomacy, 1815–1915,* Washington, 1916. This writer gives a valuable summary of the case and arrives at the following conclusion: "But the whole affair was unjustifiable. It is true that the insult to Borland and the depredations upon the property of the Transit Company demanded some action on the part of the United States government, but to bombard and then burn a town deserted by its inhabitants, and thus to destroy the property of the innocent with the guilty, was an act unworthy of a civilized nation." Williams: *op. cit.*, p. 183. See also British and Foreign State Papers, Vol. 46, pp. 859, 866–72, 875, 877, 878; Vol. 47, pp. 1012–18; Richardson: *Messages and Papers of the Presidents,* Vol. 5, p. 282; note of Mr. Marcy, Secretary of State, to the Count of Sartiges, French Minister, Feb. 26, 1857, S. Ex. Doc. No. 9, 35th Cong., 1st sess.; Moore: *Dig.*, Vol. 2, pp. 414–18.

151. President McKinley, Annual Message, Dec. 3, 1900, For. Rel. 1900, p. 8.

152. Holland, Thomas E.: *Studies in International Law,* Oxford, 1898, pp. 144–45; Hogan, Albert E.: *Pacific Blockade,* Oxford, 1908, p. 31.

153. Ducrocq: *Blocus pacifique,* Paris, 1901, p. 173. See also Hogan: *op. cit.*, pp. 66, 130–37, 142–49; Holland: *op. cit.*, p. 145; Bulmancq: *Clunet,* Vol. 11, pp. 569 *et seq.*; Heffter: *Le droit international de l'Europe,* 3d French ed., by Bergson, 1873, p. 215; Perels: *Das internationale öffentliche Seerecht der Gegenwart,* Berlin, 1903, pp. 151–55.

154. For. Rel. 1903, pp. 420, 421, 423, 452, 455, 458; Moore: *Dig.*, Vol. 4, pp. 140–41.

155. British and Foreign State Papers, Vol. 39, 1849–50 (2), pp. 217–972; Annual Register, 1850, Vol. 92, Chap. III, pp. 57–88, 281–94; Martens, Karl von: *Causes célèbres,* Vol. 5, pp. 395–531; Calvo: *op. cit.*, 4th ed., 1888, Secs. 1814, 1841; Phillimore: *op. cit.*, ed. of 1857, Vol. 3, p. 78; Bonfils: *op. cit.*, 4th ed., by Fauchille, 1905, Sec. 988; Wheaton: *Elements of International Law,* 4th English ed., 1904, Secs. 293–99; Hogan: *op. cit.*, pp. 105–14.

156. British and Foreign State Papers, Vol. 39, 1849–50 (2), pp. 538–39.

157. *Ibid.*

158. Hall: *op. cit.*, 3d ed., Oxford, 1890, Sec. 120; Westlake: *op. cit.*, ed. of 1907, Vol. 2, pp. 6–11; Westlake: *Collected Papers*, ed. by L. Oppenheim, Cambridge, 1914, pp. 590–606; Twiss: *op. cit.*, 3d French ed., Paris, 1889, Vol. 2, Secs. 11–22; Moore: *Dig.*, Vol. 7, Secs. 1095–96; Hyde: *op. cit.*, Vol. 2, Secs. 589–91, 593, 594; Pradier-Fodéré: *op. cit.*, Vol. 6, Nos. 2637–47; Macoby, S.: article in *Cambridge Law Journal*, 1924, pp. 60–73; Bluntschli: *op. cit.*, Secs. 500–504.

159. The Reports to the Hague Conferences of 1899 and 1907 . . . ed. with an Introduction by James Brown Scott, Oxford, 1917, pp. 489–99.

160. Hall: *op. cit.*, 8th ed., p. 434.

161. Oppenheim: *op. cit.*, 4th ed., by McNair, Vol. 2, p. 86.

162. Westlake: *op. cit.*, ed. of 1913, Vol. 2, pp. 126–28; Westlake: *Collected Papers*, p. 243; Oppenheim: *op. cit.*, 4th ed., by McNair, Vol. 2, p. 142; Garner: *op. cit.*, Vol. 2, Secs. 439–40; Bordwell, Percy: *The Law of War*, Chicago, 1908, pp. 100–193; Hyde: *op. cit.* Vol. 2, Sec. 655; Phillimore: *op. cit.*, 2d ed., 1873, Vol. 3, Sec. 50.

163. Holtzendorff, Franz von: *Handbuch des Völkerrechts*, 4 vols., Hamburg, 1885–89, article by Dr. Lüder, Vol. 4, pp. 253–59; Ullmann, Samuel: *Völkerrecht*, Tübingen, 1908, Sec. 170; Meurer, Christian: *Das Kriegsrecht der Haagen Konferenz*, 2 vols., München, 1907, Vol. 2, pp. 7–15. See also Visscher, Ch. de: " Les lois de la guerre et la théorie de la nécessité, *R.D.I.P.*, Vol. 24 (1917), pp. 74–108; Klüber, Jean Louis: *Droit des gens moderne de l'Europe*, ed. by M. A. Ott, Paris, 1861, Secs. 243–44; Kohler, J.: " Notwehr und Neutralität," *Z.V.*, Vol. 8, Breslau, 1914, pp. 576–78; Kaeckenbeck, Georges: in " Transactions of the Grotius Society," Vol. 4 (1919), pp. 229–30; Strupp, Karl: *Das völkerrechtliche Delikt*, Stuttgart, 1920, pp. 172–79. For a list of the German authorities, see Garner: *op. cit.*, Vol. 2, pp. 195–97.

164. Garner: *op. cit.*, Vol. 2, pp. 319–32; Cobbett: *op. cit.*, 4th ed., 1924, pp. 140–42.

165. Westlake: *op. cit.*, ed. of 1904, Vol. 1, pp. 269–99.

166. Scott: *Reports*, pp. 126, 509.

167. See, for examples, Arts. V, VIII, XXI, XXIII, XL, LII, LIII; Scott: *Reports*, pp. 127, 129, 131–32, 134–36.

168. ". . . military necessity has been taken into account in framing the Regulations, and has not been left outside them, to control and limit their application in the circumstances which they embrace." Westlake: *op. cit.*, ed. of 1907, Vol. 2, p. 57.

169. " Article I. The laws, rights and duties of war apply not only to armies, but also to militia and volunteer corps fulfilling the following conditions:

" (1) To be commended by a person responsible for his subordinates.

" (2) To have a fixed distinctive emblem recognizable at a distance.

" (3) To carry arms openly, and

" (4) To conduct their operations in accordance with the laws and customs of war." Scott: *Reports*, p. 128.

170. Scott: *Reports*, p. 128.

171. Morgan, J. H.: *The German War Book, being "The Usages of War on Land" issued by the Great General Staff of the German Army*, London, 1915, Chap. I.

172. Garner: *op. cit.*, Vol. 1, Chap. XII.

173. Scott: *Reports*, p. 519.

174. Spaight, J. M.: *War Rights on Land*, London, 1911, p. 170. See also Holland: *Studies*, pp. 106–11; Wheaton: *Elements of International Law*, ed. by Coleman Phillipson, London, 1916, pp. 508–9.

175. Spaight: *op. cit.*, p. 170.

176. Scott: *Reports*, p. 516.

177. *Ibid.*

178. Oppenheim: *op. cit.*, Vol. 2, p. 194.

179. Sherman, W. T.: *Memoirs*, 2 vols., New York, 1875, Vol. 2, p. 120.

180. Martens, G. F. von: *Précis*, p. 400; Spaight: *op. cit.*, p. 182; article by M. Arthur Desjardins in *Revue des deux mondes*, March 1, 1900, p. 52.

181. Spaight: *op. cit.*, pp. 184–86.

182. Art. XXVII; Scott: *Reports*, p. 516.

183. Pillet: "La guerre actuelle et le droit des gens," *R.D.I.P.*, 1916, Vol. 23, p. 429; Spaight: " Air Bombardment," *B.Y.I.L.*, 1923–24, pp. 23–24.

184. Spaight: *B.Y.I.L.*, 1925, p. 6.

185. *Ibid.*

186. Art. XXIV, Sec. 1, Hague Conference of 1922–23, quoted

in Moore, John Bassett: *International Law and Some Current Illusions*, New York, 1924, p. 243. Mr. Moore was a member of the conference, and in this book he reproduces the text with explanations and comments of the highest value.

187. Art. XXIV; Sec. 4; Moore: *op. cit.*, p. 243.

188. Art. XXV; Moore: *op. cit.*, p. 244.

189. Art. XXX; Moore: *op. cit.*, pp. 250–51.

190. Art. XXXV; Moore: *op. cit.*, p. 253.

191. Art. XXXVI; Moore: *op. cit.*, pp. 254–55.

192. Moore: *op. cit.*, p. 255.

193. Art. LVII; Moore: *op. cit.*, p. 282.

194. Art. LIX; Moore: *op. cit.*, pp. 282–83.

195. Art. LX; Moore: *op. cit.*, p. 283.

196. Art. XXIII, Hague Conference of 1907; Scott: *Reports*, p. 516.

197. Churchill, Winston: *The River War*, Vol. 3, pp. 195–97. He says that many dervishes had to be killed after the battle of Omdurman because they endangered the lives of those coming to help them.

198. Westlake: *op. cit.*, ed. of 1907, Vol. 2, p. 75; Spaight: *War Rights on Land*, p. 94.

199. Art. V, Hague Conference of 1907; Scott: *Reports*, p. 512.

200. Art. VIII, Hague Conference of 1907; Scott: *Reports*, p. 513.

201. Spaight: *op. cit.*, pp. 280–81.

202. Art. XXI, Hague Conference of 1907; Scott: *Reports*, p. 515.

203. Spaight: *op. cit.*, p. 419

204. Ariga, Nagao: *La guerre russo-japonaise*, Paris, 1908, pp. 132–33.

205. Spaight: *op. cit.*, p. 428. Thus in the Russo-Japanese War, the Russians were compelled to sweep 203-Metre Hill in order to prevent its capture by the Japanese, and were forced to leave the sick and wounded to their fate. Spaight points out that the action of the Russians was warranted by " the stern necessity of the defense," and that " before that necessity every other consideration had to give way." *Ibid.*, pp. 428–29.

206. This situation has occurred repeatedly in many wars: after Cold Harbor in the American Civil War (Grant: *Memoirs*, pp. 501–2); after the attack on the Tugela Heights in the Boer War (Spaight: *op. cit.*, p. 428); and at Port Arthur (*Ibid.*, p. 429).

207. This, for example, was one of the reasons that compelled the Japanese to refuse to grant such a delay after the battle of Cha-ho. Ariga: *op. cit.*, p. 167.
208. Art. V, Geneva Convention; Spaight: *op. cit.*, p. 420.
209. Oppenheim: *op. cit.*, Vol. 2, Secs. 136, 140.
210. Art. VII, Geneva Convention; Spaight: *op. cit.*, p. 436.
211. Art. VIII, Geneva Convention; Spaight: *op. cit.*, p. 436.
212. Art. IX, Geneva Convention; Spaight: *op. cit.*, p. 440.
213. Ariga: *op. cit.*, pp. 189–91.
214. Art. XV, Geneva Convention; Spaight: *op. cit.*, p. 447.
215. Art. XVII, Geneva Convention; Spaight: *op. cit.*, p. 451.
216. *Ibid.*
217. Bonfils: *op. cit.*, ed. of 1914, Sec. 1241.
218. Spaight: *op. cit.*, p. 221.
219. *Ibid.*, p. 225.
220. *Ibid.*, pp. 227–28.
221. Ariga: *op. cit.*, p. 164.
222. *Ibid.*, p. 257.
223. Spaight: *op. cit.*, p. 241.
224. Art. XXIII, Hague Rules of 1907; Scott: *Reports*, p. 516.
225. *Ibid.*
226. *Ibid.*
227. Arts. LII–LIII, Hague Rules of 1907; Scott: *Reports*, p. 520.
228. Spaight: *op. cit.*, p. 115.
229. Hall: *op. cit.*, 5th ed., p. 535. See also Dana's Wheaton, pp. 433–37; Holland: *The Laws and Customs of War*, p. 30; Spaight: *op. cit.*, p. 116; Bonfils: *op. cit.*, Sec. 1195; Bluntschli: *op. cit.*, Sec. 652; Oppenheim: *op. cit.*, Vol. 2, pp. 187, 190–91.
230. Spaight: *op. cit.*, pp. 118–27.
231. Grant: *Memoirs*, Vol. 2, p. 552; Sherman: *Memoirs*, Vol. 2, pp. 111–29.
232. Sheridan, P. H.: *Memoirs*, New York, 1888, Vol. 1, pp. 321–22.
233. Spaight: *op. cit.*, pp. 136–38.
234. Art. LII, Hague Conference of 1907; Scott: *Reports*, p. 520.
235. Sherman: *Memoirs*, Vol. 2, p. 83.
236. Destree, Jules: *The Deportation of Belgian Workmen*, London, 1917; Heuvel, J. van den: "*De la déportation des Belges en Allemagne*," *R.D.I.P.*, Vol. 24, p. 261; Toynbee, Arnold J.: *The Belgian Deportations*, London, 1917.

237. See the correspondence between Secretary Lansing and the American chargé d'affaires at Berlin, American White Book, European War, Vol. 4, pp. 357–73.

238. Despagnet: *op. cit.*, pp. 298–99.

239. *Ibid.*, p. 299.

240. *Annuaire,* Vol. 5, pp. 157, 174; Scott, James Brown: *L'institut de droit international: tableau général des travaux (1873–1913)*, New York, 1920, p. 42.

241. Hozier: *Franco-Prussian War,* Vol. 2, p. 90, quoted in Spaight: *op. cit.*, p. 467.

242. Spaight: *op. cit.*, pp. 467–68.

243. Westlake: *op. cit.*, ed. of 1907, Vol. 2, pp. 114–15.

244. Hall: *op. cit.*, 5th ed., Introduction, p. 7.

245. *Supra,* pp. 51–53. Mr. Moore cites the Greytown case in his section dealing with necessary self-defense and he also cites it under coast warfare in his chapter dealing with maritime war. See Moore: *Dig.*, Vol. 2, pp. 414–18; Vol. 7, pp. 346–54.

246. U. S. For. Rel. 1863, Part 2, pp. 1053–54.

247. Mr. Seward to Mr. Pruyn, Oct. 3, 1863, U. S. For. Rel. 1863, Part 2, p. 1016.

248. Moore: *Dig.*, Vol. 7, pp. 116–17.

249. *Supra,* pp. 83–84.

250. The Hague Rules declare that no vessel can acquire the status of a ship of war, or the rights and duties appertaining to that character, unless it is placed under the direct authority and immediate control and responsibility of the Power whose flag she flies; that such a vessel must carry all the external marks distinguishing warships belonging to her nationality; that the commander must be in the service of the state, duly commissioned, and his name placed on the official navy list; that the crew must be subject to naval discipline; that the vessel must comply with the laws and customs of war, and, finally, that in case of a conversion, it must be made the subject of a public notification as soon as possible. Arts. I–VI, Hague Conference of 1907; Scott: *Reports,* pp. 590–91.

251. Hall: *op cit.*, 2d ed., 1884, Sec. 183; Dana's Wheaton: p. 452; *The Abigail,* 4 C. Rob. 72.

252. Convention IX, Art. I, Hague Conference of 1907; Scott: *Reports,* p. 157.

253. Art. II, Hague Conference of 1907; Scott: *Reports,* pp. 157–58.

254. Art. II, Hague Conference of 1907; Scott: *Reports*, p. 158.
255. Art. III, Hague Conference of 1907; Scott: *Reports*, p. 158.
256. Art. V, Hague Conference of 1907; Scott: *Reports*, pp. 158–59.
257. *Supra*, pp. 63–68.
258. Art. VI, Hague Conference of 1907; Scott: *Reports*, p. 159.
259. ". . . having regard to the great interests entrusted to the British Navy, to the safety of peaceful commerce on the high seas, and to the maintenance within limits of international law of trade between neutral countries, the Admiralty feel it necessary to adopt exceptional measures appropriate to the novel conditions under which this war is being waged." The British Ambassador to the American Secretary of State, Nov. 3, 1914, American White Book, European War, Vol. 4, p. 30.
260. Scheer: *Germany's High Sea Fleet in the World War*, London, New York, etc., 1920, pp. 60–61; Young, Filson: *With the Battle Cruisers*, London, New York, etc., 1921, pp. 82–84; *The Times Documentary History of the War*, London, 1917, Vol. 4 ("Naval"), Part 2, pp. 237–38.
261. Garner: *op. cit.*, Vol. 1, pp. 334–38.
262. Oppenheim: *op. cit.*, 4th ed., by McNair, Vol. 2, pp. 503–6; Garner: *op. cit.*, Vol. 1, Secs. 214, 227; Int. Law Association, 29th *Report* (1920), pp. 166–73; Lawrence and Carter: in "Transactions of the Grotius Society," Vol. 1 (1916), pp. 48–49; Bonfils: *op. cit.*, ed. of 1914, Secs. 1416–21.
263. Scott: *Reports*, p. 657.
264. *Ibid.*, p. 645.
265. Art. I, Hague Conference of 1907; Scott: *Reports*, p. 645.
266. Art. II, Hague Conference of 1907; Scott: *Reports*, p. 645.
267. Art. III, Hague Conference of 1907; Scott: *Reports*, pp. 645–46.
268. *Ibid.*
269. Art. I, Hague Conference of 1907; Scott: *Reports*, p. 645.
270. Art. VI, Hague Conference of 1907; Scott: *Reports*, p. 646.
271. Garner: *op. cit.*, Vol. 1, Chap. XIV.
272. German Memorandum of February 4, 1915, enclosed in communication of Mr. Gerard, Ambassador to Germany, to Mr. Bryan, Secretary of State, Feb. 6, 1915, American White Book, European War, Vol. 1, p. 53; Herr von Jagow, German Secretary for Foreign Affairs, to Mr. Gerard, July 8, 1915, *ibid.*, Vol. 2, p. 175; Memorandum from the German Embassy filed with the

Department of State, March 8, 1916, American White Book, European War, Vol. III, pp. 184–85. For a summary of the correspondence see Hyde: *op. cit.*, Vol. 2, pp. 418–22.

273. Mr. Lansing, Secretary of State, to Mr. Gerard, Ambassador to Germany, July 21, 1915, American White Book, Vol. 2, p. 178.

274. Westlake: *Collected Papers*, ed. of 1914, pp. 254–59; Takahashi, Sakuyei: *International Law Applied to the Russo-Japanese War*, New York, 1908, p. 788; Westlake: *op. cit.*, ed. of 1913, Vol. 2, p. 309; Heffter: *op. cit.*, 4th ed., Paris, 1883, p. 317; Bluntschli: *op. cit.*, ed. of 1872, Sec. 672; Holland: *Neutral Duties in Maritime Law*, in "Proceedings of the British Academy," Vol. 2, pp. 12, 13; Atherley-Jones, L. A.: *Commerce in War*, London, 1907, pp. 528–29, 530; Dana's Wheaton: *Elements of International Law*, note 186, p. 485; Hyde: *op. cit.*, Vol. 2, pp. 496–98.

275. *Annuaire de l'Institut* (1882–83), Vol. 6, p. 221.

276. See policy announced in the communication of Count von Bernstorff, German Ambassador at Washington, to Mr. Lansing, American Secretary of State, Jan. 31, 1917, respecting submarine operations to be undertaken in waters adjacent to territories of the Allies. American White Book, European War, Vol. 4, pp. 403–5. See also Scheer: *op. cit.*, Chaps. XIII–XIV.

277. *A.J.I.L.*, Vol. 16 (1922), Supplement, p. 58.

278. Art. IV, Hague Conference of 1907; Scott: *Reports*, p. 165.

279. *Ibid.*

280. Art. IV, Hague Conference of 1907; Scott: *Reports*, p. 166.

281. *Ibid.*

282. Art. IV, Hague Conference of 1907; Scott: *Reports*, p. 167.

283. *Ibid.*

284. Art. IV, Hague Conference of 1907; Scott: *Reports*, p. 168.

285. Art. XVI, Hague Conference of 1907; Scott: *Reports*, p. 171.

286. Westlake: *Collected Papers*, ed. of 1914, pp. 249–50; Hogan: *op. cit.*, p. 42.

287. Latifi, Alma: *Effects of War on Property*, London, 1909, p. 110; *United States Service Journal*, 1855, Part 3, pp. 108–12.

288. *The Paquete Habana, The Lola*, 175 U. S. 677, 708.

289. *Supra*, p. 43.

290. Woolsey: "Proceedings," American Society of International Law, 1910, Vol. 4, p. 103.

291. For the distinction between requisition and angary see an

exhaustive article by Mr. C. Ll. Bullock in *B.Y.I.L.*, 1922–23, pp. 99–130. See also Phillimore: *op. cit.*, Vol. 3, Sec. 29; Rolin, A.: "Le droit d'angarie," *R.D.I.P.*, 3 ser., Vol. 1 (1920), p. 19; Heffter: *op. cit.*, ed. of 1883, by Geffcken, Sec. 150; Hyde: *op. cit.*, Vol. 2, p. 261; Bluntschli: *op. cit.*, ed. of 1895, Sec. 795; Westlake: *op. cit.*, Vol. 2, pp. 126–35; Oppenheim: *op. cit.*, Vol. 2, Secs. 364–67; Borchard: *Diplomatic Protection of Citizens Abroad*, p. 266; Despagnet, F.: *Cours de droit international public*, 3d ed., Paris, 1905, Sec. 494; Albrecht, Erich: Supplement to *Z.V.*, Vol. 6 (1912), "Requisitionen von neutralem Privateigentum, insbesondere von Schiffen"; Harley, J. E.: "The Law of Angary," *A.J.I.L.*, Vol. 13 (1919), pp. 267–300.

292. Colombos, Constantin John: *A Treatise on the Law of Prize*, London, 1926, p. 277.

293. Stewart's Vice-Admiralty Reports (Nova Scotia), p. 312.

294. *The Zamora*, 1916, 2 A. C. 77.

295. *The Zamora*, Law Reports, 1916, Vol. 2, p. 106.

296. Prize Cases Heard and Decided in the Prize Court . . . by the Right Hon. Sir Samuel Evans . . . and on Appeal to the Judicial Committee of the Privy Council, ed. by E. C. M. Trehern and A. W. Grant, 3 vols., London, 1916–22, Vol. 2, pp. 264–68.

297. French Prize Court in *The Rioja* (No. 2) and *The Teresa Fabregas* (1915), J. O. December 2 and 22 (1915), 8778, 9410; German Supreme Court in *The Pitea and Presto* (1918), G. A. I. (1924), 225; *The Forsete* (1918), Judgment of June 27, 1918, Rep. Fry Lib., quoted in Colombos: *Law of Prize*, p. 280.

298. Basedevant: "La réquisition des navires allemands en Portugal," *R.D.I.P.*, Vol. 23 (1916), pp. 268 ff.

299. Parl. Papers, Misc., No. 5 (1918).

300. *A.J.I.L.*, Vol. 12, Supplement, pp. 254, 260.

301. Parl. Papers (1871), 35; State Papers (1871), Vol. 81, p. 250; Albrecht, Erich: Supplement to *Z.V.* (1912), Vol. 6, "Requisitionen von neutralem Privateigentum, insbesondere von Schiffen," pp. 24–66.

302. British and Foreign State Papers, 61 (1870–1871), pp. 580–81.

303. *Ibid.*, pp. 575–78, 611–12.

304. Art. XIX, Hague Conference of 1907; Scott: *Reports*, p. 536.

305. *The Maria*, I. C. Rob. 340, 374.

306. *Ibid.*

307. Memorandum issued by the Department of State, Sept. 19, 1914, American White Book, European War, Vol. 2, p. 43; Scott, J. B.: *Survey of International Relations between the United States and Germany*, New York, 1917, pp. 247–64; Hyde: *op. cit.*, Vol. 2, pp. 468–72.

308. Hall: *op. cit.*, 4th ed., p. 763; 5th ed., p. 735. See also *The Acteon* (1815), 3 Dods. 48; *The Leucade* (1855), Spinks, 217.

309. Moore: *Dig.*, Vol. 7, pp. 522–23.

310. Bentwich, Norman: *Law of Private Property on Land and Sea*, London, 1907, p. 104.

311. *The Knight Commander*, Hurst, C. J. B., and Bray, F. E.: *Russian and Japanese Prize Cases*, London, 1912–13, Vol. 1, pp. 54, 357; Woolsey, Theodore S.: "The Knight Commander Case," *Yale Law Journal*, Vol. 16, p. 566; Foreign Relations, 1904, pp. 734–35.

312. Smith, Sir Frederick: *The Destruction of Merchant Ships in International Law*, London, 1917, p. 95.

313. The Declaration of London declared that it is the normal duty of a captor not to destroy a neutral prize, but added that where the captured vessel was itself liable to condemnation, it might be destroyed if the failure to take such action would involve danger to the safety of the vessel, or the success of the operations in which it was then engaged. The captor resorting to such procedure must, however, prior to any discussion respecting the validity of the prize, establish that he acted in the face of an extraordinary necessity. Arts. XLVIII and LI of the Declaration of London. See Hyde: *op. cit.*, Vol. 2, pp. 512–13.

314. See Art. XL, Russian Instructions, in Proceedings Relating to Capture, Sept. 20, 1900, Hurst and Bray: *op. cit.*, Vol. 1, p. 339.

315. Art. CXIII of the Prize Code of 1914 instructed naval officers to destroy neutral prizes for contraband tradings, violations of blockade, or unneutral service, if to take them in for adjudication might endanger the captor's safety or the success of his operations. Huberich, C. H., and King, R.: *The Prize Code of the German Empire*, New York, 1915, p. 66.

316. The United States Naval Instructions Governing Maritime Warfare, of June 30, 1917, No. 96, contemplate such procedure in case the officer making the capture is confronted with "the gravest military emergency which would not justify him in releas-

ing the vessel or sending it in for adjudication." Quoted in Hyde: *op. cit.*, Vol. 2, p. 503.

317. Smith, Sir Frederick: *op. cit.*, pp. 76–78. See also Sir Edward Fry: " The Rights of Neutrals as Illustrated by Recent Events," in " Proceedings of the British Academy," Vol. 2, London, 1906, p. 3.

318. Smith, Sir Frederick: *op. cit.*, pp. 76–78.

319. *Supra*, pp. 100–101.

320. *Supra*, p. 102.

321. Atherley-Jones, L. A.: *op. cit.*, p. 537; Lord Lansdowne to Sir C. Hardinge, British Ambassador to Russia, August 10, 1904, Parl. Papers, Russia, No. 1 (1905), pp. 11, 12.

322. Atherley-Jones, L. A.: *op. cit.*, p. 537.

323. *Annuaire* (1913), Vol. 26, p. 348.

324. Naval War College, International Law Topics, 1905, p. 62.

325. Moore: *Int. Arb.*, Vol. 2, p. 1096.

326. " Considering, in this state of things, that Captain Reid, not having applied, in the beginning, for the intervention of the Neutral Sovereign, and having had recourse to arms for the purpose of repelling an unjust aggression of which he claimed to be the object, thus failed to respect the neutrality of the territory of the foreign sovereign, and released that sovereign from the obligation to afford him protection by any other means than that of a pacific intervention." From the text of the award. Quoted in Moore: *Int. Arb.*, Vol. 2, p. 1096. " The only international question actually decided in the case of the *General Armstrong* is that a vessel which, in anticipation of a hostile attack, prepares to resist it by force, and does so resist it, without applying to the neutral sovereign for protection, can not afterwards hold such a sovereign responsible for his injuries." Statement of Mr. Moore. Moore: *Dig.*, Vol. 7, p. 1095.

327. Moore: *Int. Arb.*, Vol. 2, p. 1132.

328. Moore: *Dig.*, Vol. 1, pp. 252–54; Moore: *Int. Arb.*, Vol. 5, p. 4473.

329. Moore: *Dig.*, Vol. 7, p. 1053.

330. *Ibid.*

331. Wheaton: *op. cit.*, 5th ed., 1916, p. 641; Vattel: *op. cit.*, Book III, Sec. 122; Bluntschli: *op. cit.*, Sec. 782; Calvo: *op. cit.*, Vol. 4, Sec. 2642; Oppenheim: *op. cit.*, 4th ed., by McNair, Vol. 2, p. 519.

332. *The Anna*, 5 C. Rob. 385.

333. Hansard: n.s., Vol. 23, p. 737; Vol. 24 (1830), p. 126; Phillimore: *op. cit.*, Vol. 3, p. 296.

334. *The Düsseldorf*, 3 B. and C. P. C. (1920), 664, A. C. 1034; *The Anne*, 3 Wheat. 435; *The Diligentia*, 1 Dods. 404; *The Eliza Ann*, 2 Dods. 244; *The Florida*, 104 U. S. 37.

335. Art. XIII, Hague Convention of 1907.

336. *The Düsseldorf*, 3 B. and C. P. C. 664; *The Sir William Peel*, in Moore: *Int. Arb.*, Vol. 4, p. 3935.

337. *The Pellworm*, 3 B. and C. P. C. 702, 1053; The *Valeria*, 3 B. and C. P. C. (1921), 834, A. C. 477; Colombos: *op. cit.*, pp. 108–16.

338. *The Ryeshitelni*, in Takahashi: *op. cit.*, p. 437; United States For. Rel. 1904, p. 139; Birkenhead, F. E. Smith, First Earl of, and Sibley, N. W.: *International Law as Interpreted during the Russo-Japanese War*, London, 1917, pp. 116–19.

339. Parl. Papers, 1915, Cd. 1859; Garner: *op. cit.*, Vol. 2, Sec. 562.

340. "Necessity knows no law. Our troops have occupied Luxemburg and perhaps are already on Belgian soil. Gentlemen, that is contrary to the dictates of international law. It is true that the French Government has declared at Brussels that France is willing to respect the neutrality of Belgium as long as her opponent respects it. We knew, however, that, France stood ready for the invasion. France could wait but we could not wait. A French movement upon our flanks upon the lower Rhine might have been disastrous. So we were compelled to override the just protest of the Luxemburg and Belgian Governments. The wrong — I speak openly — that we are committing we will endeavor to make good as soon as our military goal has been reached, Anybody who is threatened as we are threatened, and is fighting for his highest possessions, can have only one thought — how he is to hack his way through." Stowell, Ellery C.: *Diplomacy of the War of 1914*, New York, 1915, p. 445, note 2.

341. Scott, J. B.: *Diplomatic Documents Relating to the Outbreak of the European War;* Hyde: *op. cit.*, Vol. 2, p. 790; Renault, Louis: *The First Violations of the Law of Nations by Germany: Luxemburg and Belgium*, Paris, 1917; Visscher, Ch. de: *Belgium's Case: A Juridical Enquiry*, translated from the French by E. F. Jourdain, London, 1916; Oppenheim: *op. cit.*, 4th ed., by McNair, Vol. 2, pp. 147, 508; Garner: *op. cit.*, Secs. 431–52.

342. Stowell, Ellery C.: *Intervention*, Washington, 1921, pp. 409–14; Senior, Nassau: article in *Edinburgh Review*, April, 1843, Vol. 15, p. 328; *Letters of the First Earl of Malmesbury*, London, 1870, Vol. 2, p. 51. For a defense of the British point of view see Westlake: *op. cit.*, Vol. 1, pp. 302–3; Hall: *op. cit.*, 4th ed., pp. 285–87. Hall declares that: "The emergency was one which gave good reason for the general line of conduct of the English government." He admits, however, that "Denmark, in the exercise of an indubitable right, chose to look upon its action as hostile." *Ibid.*, pp. 286–87.

343. Parliamentary Debates, House of Commons, 5th ser., Vol. 74, pp. 1514–15. See also Ion, Theodore P.: "The Hellenic Crisis," *A J I L.*, Vol. 12, pp. 562–88.

344. Oppenheim: *op. cit.*, 4th ed., by McNair, Vol. 2, p. 513.

345. Parliamentary Debates, Vol. 81, pp. 2184–85. Quoted in Ion: *op. cit.*, *A J I L.*, Vol. 12, pp. 566–67.

346. *The Times* (London), April 12, 1916. Quoted in Ion: *op. cit.*, Vol. 12, p. 575.

347. *The Tinos*, etc., J. O., Jan. 9, 1918, p. 401. Quoted in Colombos *op. cit.*, p. 118; Ion: *op. cit.*, Vol. 12, p. 584.

348. Abbott, G. F.: *Turkey, Greece and the Great Powers*, London, 1916, Chap. VII. This writer makes out a very good case for the efforts of King Constantine to maintain neutrality.

349. Dane, Edmund: *British Campaigns in the Near East, 1914–1918*, London and New York, 1918, 2 vols., Vol. 2, pp. 1–5; Marriott, J. A. R.: *The Eastern Question*, Oxford, 1924, pp. 497–500.

350. Bau, Mingchieu Joshua: *The Foreign Relations in China: A History and Survey*, New York, 1921, pp. 427–28.

351. For an exhaustive discussion of the case, see Tchen, Hoshien: *Étude sur les relations diplomatiques entre la Chine et le Japon de 1871 à nos jours*, Paris, 1921, pp. 152–68. The writer of this treatise maintains that the plea of military necessity advanced by Japan against China was wholly without foundation. See also Elliott, Charles B.: "The Shantung Question," *A J I L.*, Vol. 13 (1919), pp. 706–7; Wood, G. Zay: *The Twenty-one Demands*, New York, 1921, pp. 11–21; Wood. G. Zay: *The Shantung Question*, New York, 1922, Chap. IV; Treat, Payson J.: *Japan and the United States*, Boston, 1921, Chap. XI. For a general discussion of the right of a belligerent to invade a neutral territory for the purpose of checking a dangerous agency directed

against itself, see Phillimore: *op. cit.*, Vol. 1, Secs. 210–20; Vattel: *op. cit.*, Book II, Chap. VII; Calvo: *op. cit.*, Vol. I, Secs. 208–9; Klüber: *op. cit.*, Sec. 44; Twiss: *op. cit.*, Vol. 1, Sec. 102; Pradier-Fodéré: *op. cit.*, Vol. 1, p. 95; Rivier: *op. cit.*, Vol. 1, Sec. 20; Despagnet: *op. cit.*, Sec. 20; Bonfils: *op. cit.*, Sec. 242.

352. *Supra*, pp. 111–112.

353. *Supra*, p. 107.

354. Moore: *Int. Arb.*, Vol. 1, p. 671.

355. Art. XXV, Sec. XIII, Hague Conference of 1907.

356. Oppenheim: *op. cit.*, Vol. 2, p. 393.

BIBLIOGRAPHY

I. DOCUMENTARY SOURCES

American and British Claims Arbitration under the Special Agreement of August 18, 1910. Report of Fred K. Nielson. Washington, 1926.

American White Book, European War. Washington, Government Printing Office, 1915.

Archives Diplomatiques. Recueil de diplomatie et d'histoire. Paris, 1861.

British and Foreign State Papers, 1812–1919.

Case of the United States in the Alabama Claims. Geneva edition.

Cobbett, Pitt: Leading Cases on International Law. 4th edition, by Hugh H. L. Bellot. London, 1922–24.

Evans, Lawrence B.: Leading Cases on International Law. Chicago, 1922.

Fur Seal Arbitration: Proceedings of the Tribunal of Arbitration. 15 vols. Washington, Government Printing Office, 1895.

Grant, Albert W.: Prize Cases Heard and Decided in Prize Court during the Great War by the Right Hon. Sir Samuel Evans. 3 vols. London, 1916–22.

Hague Arbitration Cases, The. Edited by George Grafton Wilson. Boston and London, 1915.

Hertslet, Edward: A Complete Collection of the Treaties and Conventions . . . between Great Britain and Foreign Powers. London, 1827.

Hurst, C. J. B., and Bray, F. E.: Russian and Japanese Prize Cases. London, 1912–13.

Lloyd's Reports of Prize Cases Heard before and Decided by the Right Hon. Sir Samuel Evans during the European War. Edited by J. B. Aspinwall. 10 vols. London, 1915–24.

Malloy, William M.: Treaties, Conventions, International Acts, Protocols and Agreements between the United States of America and Other Powers, 1776–1909. Washington, 1910–23.

Moore, John Bassett: A Digest of International Law. 8 vols. Washington, Government Printing Office, 1906.
Moore, John Bassett: A History and Digest of the International Arbitrations to Which the United States Has Been a Party. 6 vols. Washington, Government Printing Office, 1898.
Official Journal, League of Nations.
Papers Relating to the Foreign Relations of the United States. Washington, 1862–1916.
Recueil des decisions des tribunaux arbitraux mixtes institués par les traités de paix. Paris, 1922–25.
Scott, James Brown: Cases on International Law. St. Paul, 1922.
Scott, James Brown: Diplomatic Documents relating to the Outbreak of the European War. New York, 1916.
Scott, James Brown: L'institut de droit international: tableau général des travaux (1873–1913). New York, 1920.
Scott, James Brown: Texts of the Peace Conferences at The Hague, 1899 and 1907, with English translation and appendix of related documents. Boston, 1908.
Scott, James Brown: United States Reports, Supreme Court: Prize Cases Decided in the United States Supreme Court, 1879-1918. Oxford, 1923.
Stewart, James: Nova Scotia Reports, Vice-Admiralty Court.
Takahashi, Sakuyei: Cases on International Law during the Chino-Japanese War. Cambridge, 1899.
Times, The: Documentary History of the World War. London, 1914–18.
Wharton, Francis: A Digest of the International Law of the United States. 3 vols. Washington, Government Printing Office, 1887.
Wharton, Francis: Revolutionary Diplomatic Correspondence of the United States. Edited by Francis Wharton. 6 vols. Washington, Government Printing Office, 1889.

II. MONOGRAPHS

Abbott, G. F.: Turkey, Greece and the Great Powers. London, 1916.
Albrecht, Adolf E.: Requisitionen von neutralem Privateigentum, insbesondere von Schiffen. Breslau, 1912.
Ariga, Nagao: La guerre russo-japonaise. Paris, 1908.
Atherley-Jones, L. A.: Commerce in War. London, 1907.

Bau, Mingchieu Joshua: The Foreign Relations of China: A History and Survey. New York, 1921.

Benedict, Erastus C.: The American Admiralty. Albany, 1910.

Birkenhead, F. E. Smith, First Earl of: The Destruction of Merchant Ships under International Law. London, 1917.

Birkenhead, F. E. Smith, First Earl of, and Sibley, N. W.: International Law as Interpreted during the Russo-Japanese War. London, 1907.

Borchard, Edwin M.: The Diplomatic Protection of Citizens Abroad. New York, 1916.

Bordwell, Percy: The Law of War between Belligerents. Chicago, 1908.

Bynkershoek, Cornelius van: A Treatise on the Law of War. English translation by Peter Stephen du Ponceau. Philadelphia, 1810.

Bynkershoek, Cornelius van: De dominio maris dissertatio. English translation by R. V. D. Magoffin. New York, 1923.

Catellani, Enrico L.: Condozioni e effetti grundica dello stato di guerra. Venice, 1906.

Colombos, Constantin John: A Treatise on the Law of Prize. London, 1926.

Dane, Edmund: British Campaigns in the Near East, 1914–18. 2 vols. London and New York, 1918.

Despagnet, F.: La guerre sud-africaine au point de vue du droit international. Paris, 1902.

Destree, Jules: The Deportation of Belgian Workmen. London, 1917.

Ducrocq, Robert: Blocus pacifique. Paris, 1901.

Fulton, Thomas Wemyss: The Sovereignty of the Sea. Edinburgh and London, 1911.

Garner, J. W.: International Law and the World War. 2 vols. New York, 1920.

Gentili, Alberico: Hispanicae Advocationis. English translation by Frank Frost Abbott. New York, 1921.

Goebel, Julius, Jr.: The Equality of States. New York, 1923.

Grotius, Hugo: The Freedom of the Seas. English translation by R. V. D. Magoffin. New York, 1916.

Hershey, Amos S.: Diplomatic Agents and Immunities. Washington, 1919.

Hershey, Amos S.: The International Law and Diplomacy of the Russo-Japanese War. New York, 1906.

Hogan, Albert E.: Pacific Blockade. Oxford, 1908.
Latifi, Alma: Effects of War on Property. London, 1909.
Machiavelli, Niccolò: Discourse on the First Decade of Titus Livius. English translation by Ninian Hill Thompson. London, 1883.
Marriott, J. A. R.: The Eastern Question. Oxford, 1924.
Meurer, Christian: Das Gastrecht der Schiffe im Krieg und Frieden. Berlin, 1918.
Meurer, Christian: Das Kriegsrecht der Haager Konferenz. 2 vols. Munich, 1907.
Morley, John: Critical Miscellanies, Vol. 4: Machiavelli. New York, 1908.
Parton, James: Life of Andrew Jackson. New York, 1860.
Phillipson, Coleman: International Law and the Great War. London, 1915.
Piggott, Sir Francis T.: Nationality. London, 1907.
Renault, Louis: The First Violations of the Law of Nations by Germany: Luxemburg and Belgium. Paris, 1917.
Satow, Sir Ernest M.: A Guide to Diplomatic Practice. London, 1917.
Scheer, Admiral: Germany's High Sea Fleet in the World War. London and New York, 1920.
Scott, J. B.: Survey of International Relations between the United States and Germany. New York, 1917.
Sheridan, P. H.: Personal Memoirs. New York, 1888.
Spaight, J. M.: Aircraft and Commerce in War. New York, 1926.
Spaight, J. M.: War Rights on Land. London, 1911.
Stowell, Ellery C.: Diplomacy of the War of 1914. New York, 1915.
Stowell, Ellery C.: Intervention. Washington, 1921.
Strupp, Karl: Das völkerrechtliche Delikt. Stuttgart, 1920.
Takahashi, Sakuyei: International Law Applied to the Russo-Japanese War. New York, 1908.
Tchen, Hoshien: Étude sur les relations diplomatiques entre la Chine et la Japon de 1871 à nos jours. Paris, 1921.
Toynbee, Arnold J.: The Belgium Deportations. London, 1917.
Visscher, Ch. de: Belgium's Case: A Juridical Enquiry. Translated from the French by E. F. Jourdain. London, 1916.
Westlake, John: Collected Papers on Public International Law. Cambridge, 1914.

Wharton, Francis: A Treatise on the Conflict of Laws. Third edition, by George H. Parmele. Rochester, 1905.
Williams, Mary Wilhelmine: Anglo-American Isthmian Diplomacy, 1815–1915. Washington, 1916.
Wood, G. Zay: The Shantung Question. New York, 1922.
Wood, G. Zay: The Twenty-one Demands. New York, 1921.
Young, Filson: With the Battle Cruisers. London and New York, 1921.

III. SERIAL PUBLICATIONS

A. Titles and Abbreviations

American Journal of International Law	A. J. I. L.
Annuaire de l'Institut de Droit International	Annuaire
British Year-Book of International Law	B. Y. I. L.
Cambridge Law Journal	
Columbia Law Review	
Harvard Law Review	
International Law Association	I. L. A.
Journal du droit international privé	Clunet
Michigan Law Review	
Proceedings of the American Society of International Law	Pro. Am. Soc.
Proceedings of the British Academy	
Revue de droit international et de legislation comparée	R. D. I. L. C.
Revue générale de droit international public	R. D. I. P.
Transactions of the Grotius Society	
Yale Law Journal	
Zeitschrift für Völkerrecht und Bundesstaatsrecht	Z. V.

B. Leading Articles Cited

Basedevant, J.: La réquisition des navires allemands en Portugal. R. D. I. P., Vol. 23, 1916, pp. 268–79.
Bullock, C. Ll.: Angary. B. Y. I. L., 1922–23, pp. 99–129.
Elliott, Charles B.: The Shantung Question. A. J. I. L., Vol. 13, pp. 706–7.
Fiore, Pasquale: Délits commis à l'étranger. R. D. I. L. C., Vol. 11, pp. 302–19.
Goebel, Julius, Jr.: The Equality of States. Columbia Law Review, Vol. 23, pp. 274 ff.

Gregory, C. N.: Jurisdiction over Foreign Ships in Territorial Waters. Michigan Law Review, February, 1904, pp. 333–47.

Harley, J. E.: The Law of Angary. A. J. I. L., Vol. 13 (1919), pp. 267–311.

Heuvel, J. van den: De la déportation des Belges en Allemagne. R. D. I. P., Vol. 24, 261–300.

Holland, Thomas E.: Neutral Duties in Maritime War. Proceedings of the British Academy. Vol. 2, pp. 12 ff.

Ion, Theodore P.: The Hellenic Crisis. A. J. I. L., Vol. 12, pp. 561–88.

Kaeckenbeck, Georges: Military Necessity. Transactions of the Grotius Society, Vol. 4 (1919), pp. 229–30.

Kohler, J.: Notwehr und Neutralität. Z. V., Vol. 8, Breslau, 1914, pp. 576–78.

Maccoby, S.: Reprisals as a Means of Redress Short of War. Cambridge Law Journal, Vol. 2 (1926), pp. 60–73.

Pillet, Antoine: La guerre actuelle et la droit des gens. R. D. I. P., Vol. 23 (1916), pp. 423–71.

Root, Elihu: The Real Monroe Doctrine. A. J. I. L., Vol. 8, pp. 427–42.

Spaight, J. M.: Air Bombardment. B. Y. I. L., 1923–24, pp. 23–24.

Visscher, Ch. de: Les lois de la guerre et la théorie de la nécessité. R. D. I. P., Vol. 24 (1917), pp. 74–108.

Woolsey, Theodore S.: Effect of the Unfriendly Act of Inequitable Conduct of the Citizen upon the Right to Protection. Pro. Am. Soc., Vol. 4 (1910), pp. 99–110.

Woolsey, Theodore S.: The Knight Commander Case. Yale Law Journal, Vol. 16, pp. 566 ff.

Wright, Quincy: Territorial Propinquity. A. J. I. L., Vol. 12, pp. 519–61.

IV. GENERAL WORKS

Adams, Henry: History of the United States. 9 vols. New York, 1891–98.

Bluntschli, Johann K.: Das moderne Völkerrecht der civilisirten Staaten. Nördlingen, 1868.

Bluntschli, Johann K.: Le droit international codifié. Fifth edition, Paris, 1895.

Bluntschli, Johann K.: Le droit public général. Second edition, Paris, 1885.

Bonfils, Henry: Manuel de droit international public. Seventh edition, Paris, 1914.
Calvo, Cailos: Le droit international theorique et pratique. Fifth edition, Paris, 1869.
Creasy, Sir Edward S.: First Platform of International Law. London, 1876.
Despagnet, F.: Droit international public. Third edition, Paris, 1905.
Fauchille, Paul: Traité de droit international public. Paris, 1921.
Fenwick, Charles G.: International Law. New York, 1924.
Fiore, Pasquale: International Law Codified and Its Legal Sanction. English translation from the fifth Italian edition, with an Introduction by Edwin M. Borchard. New York, 1918.
Foster, John W.: Diplomatic Memoirs. Boston, 1909.
Grotius, Hugo: De jure belli ac pacis. English translation by A. C. Campbell. London, 1814. English translation by William Whewell. Cambridge, 1853.
Grotius, Hugo: Introduction to Dutch Jurisprudence. English translation by Charles Herbert. London, 1845.
Hall, William Edward: A Treatise on International Law. Seventh edition, by A. Pierce Higgins. Oxford, 1917.
Halleck, H. W.: International Law. Fourth edition, by Sir G. Sherston Baker. London, 1908.
Hassall, Arthur: The Foreign Policy of Louis XIV (1661–97). The Cambridge Modern History, Vol. 5, New York, 1912.
Heffter, A. W.: Das europäische Völkerrecht. Berlin, 1888.
Hobbes, Thomas: The Elements of Law, Natural and Political. Edited by Ferdinand Tönnies. London, 1878.
Hobbes, Thomas: Works. Edited by Sir William Molesworth. London, 1839–45.
Holland, Thomas E.: Studies in International Law. Oxford, 1898.
Holtzendorff, Franz: Handbuch des Völkerrechts. Berlin, 1885–89.
Hyde, Charles Cheyney: International Law Chiefly as Interpreted and Applied by the United States. 2 vols. Boston, 1922.
Kent, James: Commentary on International Law. Edited by J. T. Abdy. Second edition. Cambridge, 1878.
Klüber, Johann L.: Droit des gens moderne de l'Europe. Second edition. Paris, 1874.
Macdonell, Sir John, and Manson, Edward: Great Jurists of the World. Boston, 1914.

Machiavelli, Niccolò: Works. Translated by Ellis Farneworth. Second edition. London, 1775.

Martens, G. F. von: A Compendium of the Law of Nations. English translation by William Cobbett. London, 1802.

Martens, G. F. von: Précis du droit des gens moderne de l'Europe. Second edition. Paris, 1864.

Martens, Karl von: Causes célèbres du droit des gens, rédigées par le Bn. Charles de Martens. Second edition. Leipzig, 1858–61.

Montesquieu, Charles Louis de Secondat: The Spirit of Laws. English translation, with commentary, by Thomas Nugent. London, 1902.

Moore, John Bassett: International Law and Some Current Illusions. New York, 1924.

Moore, John Bassett: The Principles of American Diplomacy. New York, 1918.

Nys, Ernest: Le droit international. Bruxelles, 1912.

Oppenheim, L.: International Law. Second edition. London, 1912. Third edition, by R. F. Roxburgh. London, 1920–21. Fourth edition by Arnold D. McNair. London, 1926.

Ortolan, Théodore: Règles internationales et diplomatie de la mer. 2 vols. Paris, 1864.

Perels, Ferdinand: Das internationale öffentliche Seerecht der Gegenwart. Berlin, 1882.

Phillimore, Sir Robert: Commentaries upon International Law. Third edition. London, 1879–89.

Pradier-Fodéré, Paul: Traité de droit international public. Paris, 1885–1906.

Pufendorf, Samuel: De jure naturae et gentium. Frankfort and Leipzig, 1759. English translation by Basil Kennett. Oxford, 1710.

Rachel, Samuel: De jure naturae et gentium dissertationes. Edited by Ludwig von Bar. Washington, 1916. English translation by John Pawley Bate. Washington, 1916.

Rivier, Alphonse: Principes du droit des gens. Paris, 1896.

Rousseau, Jean Jacques: Political Writings. Edited by C. E. Vaughan. Cambridge, 1915.

Sherman, W. T.: Memoirs. 2 vols. New York, 1875.

Taylor, Hannis: A Treatise on International Public Law. Chicago, 1901.

Textor, Johann Wolfgang: Synopsis juris gentium. Edited by

Ludwig von Bar. Washington, 1916. English translation by John Pawley Bate. Washington, 1916.
Twiss, Sir Travers: The Law of Nations Considered as Independent Political Communities. Second edition. Oxford, 1875.
Ullmann, Samuel: Völkerrecht. Tübingen, 1908.
Vattel, Emmerich de: The Law of Nations. Sixth American edition, by Joseph Chitty. Philadelphia, 1847. English translation by Charles G. Fenwick. Washington, 1916.
Ward, Robert: An Inquiry into the Foundation and History of the Law of Nations in Europe. London, 1795.
Webster, Daniel: Works. Twelfth edition. Boston, 1860.
Westlake, John: International Law. Second edition. Cambridge, 1910–13.
Wheaton, Henry: Elements of International Law. Eighth edition, by Richard Henry Dana. London, 1866.
Wheaton, Henry: History of the Law of Nations in Europe and America. New York, 1845.
Wolff, Christian: Jus gentium methodo scientifico pertractatum. Magdeburg, 1749.
Zouche, Richard: Juris et iudicii fecialis. Edited by Thomas Erskine Holland. Washington, 1911. English translation by J. L. Brierly. Washington, 1911.

TABLE OF CASES

INDEX

COLUMBIA UNIVERSITY PRESS
Columbia University
New York

FOREIGN AGENT
OXFORD UNIVERSITY PRESS
HUMPHREY MILFORD
Amen House
London, E.C.

Bei Fragen zur Produktsicherheit wenden Sie sich bitte an:
If you have any questions regarding product safety,
please contact:

Walter de Gruyter GmbH
Genthiner Straße 13
10785 Berlin
productsafety@degruyterbrill.com